CIRCULAR WALKS IN
NORTH EASTERN WALES

Circular Walks
in North Eastern Wales

Jim Grindle

ISBN: 0-86381-550-2

Cover design: Alan Jones

First published in 1999 by
Gwasg Carreg Gwalch, 12 Iard yr Orsaf, Llanrwst, Wales LL26 0EH
℡ 01492 642031   🖷 01492 641502
✆ books@carreg-gwalch.co.uk   Web site: www.carreg-gwalch.co.uk

This book is dedicated to Margaret Davies, 1910-1998,
who loved the simple things of the countryside
but was never able to walk among them.

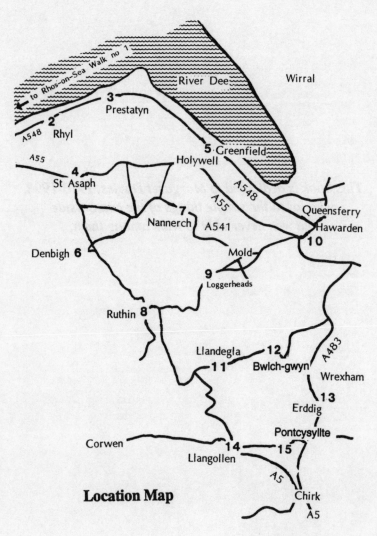

Location Map

(Note: North is at the TOP of all the maps in this guide-book)

Contents

Introduction

This book describes fifteen walks in north eastern Wales in what was until recently the county of Clwyd, now split between Denbighshire, Flintshire, Wrexham and Conwy.

Those who know this area have a great affection for it. For most holidaymakers though, it is only the background to the famous seaside resorts of northern Wales, whilst hillwalkers generally just drive through on their way to the higher mountains of Snowdonia.

I hope that this book will persuade you that there is a lot to be gained by spending some time here enjoying the beautiful landscape, and exploring the towns and villages with their rich historical background. If you are on holiday here, then you will find more than enough to keep you busy for a fortnight and still have time to spend on the beach.

Finding your way around the book

The fifteen walks can be found on the location map numbered from north to south and from left to right. Number one is Rhos-on-sea, the most northerly and on the left; number fifteen is Pontcysyllte, the most southerly and on the right.

Alphabetically they are:

Bwlch-gwyn	Walk no. 12
Denbigh	Walk no. 6
Erddig	Walk no. 13
Hawarden	Walk no. 10
Holywell	Walk no. 5
Llandegla	Walk no. 11
Llangollen	Walk no. 14
Loggerheads	Walk no. 9
Nannerch	Walk no. 7
Pontcysyllte	Walk no. 15
Prestatyn	Walk no. 3
Rhos-on-sea	Walk no. 1

Rhyl	Walk no. 2
Ruthin	Walk no. 8
St Asaph	Walk no. 4

As the text is in English I have used the English version of the names of the towns; on the Ordnance Survey maps are both the Welsh and the English place-names.

Each walk description has four parts. The first is a table of information; the second is a short commentary and outline of what the walk is about; the third describes the walk itself; and the fourth is entirely background information which may be legend, history, geology, industrial or anything else that is relevant.

The table of information begins with the walk number and a title. This is followed by a map number. All the walks in this book are on one of two Ordnance Survey Landranger maps: either sheet 116 or 117. However, during the course of the next twelve months two new maps covering NE Wales will be available in the Explorer series. These maps are twice the scale of the Landranger and are highly recommended. Always have the relevant map with you. The sheet numbers are 264, which will cover the coast down to Llangollen, and 265 which covers the Clwydian range.

The start of the walk is described and there is also a Grid Reference (GR in the text). When you buy your map look at the information down the right hand side. You will find a box headed 'How to give a grid reference (British National Grid)'. This tells you how to use the numbered lines across the map to pinpoint a location and it is the system that I have used. There follows some indication of what facilities are available by way of toilets, refreshments etc. and some pointers to public transport. Lastly you will find the length of the walk and the total height gain. In case you misunderstand, the amount of climbing is the total of all the climbs and the little ascents that you meet on the walk. Don't think that you will have to do it all in one go – a lot of it you won't even notice.

The use of jargon has been kept to a minimum but if you are not familiar with maps and walking then you deserve a few explanations. I use the abbreviation 'OS' meaning 'Ordnance Survey', the government map-making organisation. I also use the term 'OS trig point' or 'triangulation station'. These are concrete columns about 1.25m/4' high with a number plate on the side and metal fittings on top for fastening surveying instruments. Although they have been outdated in the last ten years by satellite surveying they are still on the maps, and are very useful features on the ground for walkers, especially on misty mountain tops. The only other abbreviations are km for kilometre and m for metre. The expression 'waymarking' is fairly clear but you might not be aware of the official system: yellow arrows for footpaths (pedestrians only); blue arrows for bridleways (pedestrians, horseriders and cyclists); white arrows for a path where access is by permission of the landowner. Red arrows are for byways, but these are not common.

I have taken a lot of care to make the walk descriptions accurate and as the reader sees it. The routes were all walked very recently. Things do not remain constant on the ground though, and if you come across any changes, then it would be helpful if you wrote to me via the publisher so that I can check it out for future reference.

In the text you will find numbers which refer you to the background notes (Points of Interest). I have kept these quite separate as some of them are lengthy and might confuse the directions given for the walk.

What you need to take on a walk

If you are an experienced walker then you won't need advice from me. If you haven't done a lot of walking in the countryside, then you might like a few ideas. Most of these walks are not too long, so you won't need to take huge amounts of food and drink with you. Only walks 3, 7 and 9 go to any great height so real mountain gear is not necessary but you need to keep an eye on the weather and make sure that you are going to be comfortable. In Wales this usually means being warm and dry. By now you will have gathered that a small rucksack might be a good idea, especially if you also carry binoculars, a camera and a few simple items of first aid. Take a compass if you know how to use it but it shouldn't really be necessary. You will probably manage these walks in trainers but the ground can be muddy and I always prefer boots. For these walks I found a pair of fabric lightweights were fine.

In conclusion

Although the traditional industries of coal mining and iron working are now in the past, much of this area is still industrialised and is second only to the south of the country in population and wealth. Indeed, this has always been the case. There is a lot more to north eastern Wales than buckets and spades. I do hope that you will enjoy your exploration of this lovely corner of Wales and come to appreciate how much of the history of Wales and England are interwoven in these rolling hills and beautiful valleys with their limestone outcrops, heather and gorse, castles and above all, welcoming people.

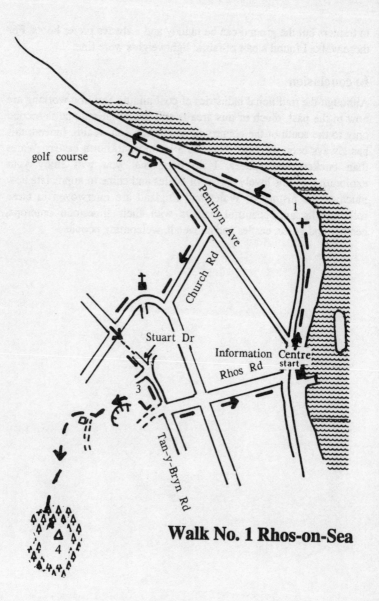

golf course

2

Penrhyn Ave

Church Rd

1

Stuart Dr

Information Centre
start

Rhos Rd

3

Tan-y-Bryn Rd

4

Walk No. 1 Rhos-on-Sea

Rhos – The discovery of America

OS Map No.:	116
Start:	G.R. 842805. The Information Centre on the prom at Rhos.
Access:	Colwyn Bay is on the Chester/Holyhead railway, National Express buses from London and the 12/13 and 16 services run along the coast road. Plenty of street car parking.
Facilities:	Toilets by the Information Centre. Numerous cafés and shops nearby. Pub at start and two on the route.

Amount of climbing: 131m/400ft.

Although this walk is largely suburban in character it does have good sea views and passes some interesting historic sites. The little hill of Bryn Euryn has better views of Snowdonia than most of the others in the book and itself makes the walk worth doing.

Walk Directions: (-) denotes Point of Interest

Walk along the Marine Drive with the sea on your right. There are several parallel pathways, the lowest of which keeps you away from the traffic and leads to the tiny chapel of St Trillo (1) at Rhos Point, surely a candidate for the smallest in Wales.

About half a mile further you are on an elevated walkway with the headland of Little Orme's Head in view. Cross the road to a large house set back from the road and situated right next to the golf course. It is called Odstone. In its garden are two pools and on the left a rockery on a huge old wall. The pools are what remains of the bed of the Afon Ganol, whilst the wall was a quay. An inscribed slate tablet on the wall faces away from the road but you can just see it. It tells us that it was from this point that Prince Madoc sailed and discovered America (2).

From here reverse direction and fork right on Penrhyn Avenue. When you reach a major crossroads where there are some shops, turn right onto Church Road which goes uphill. Turn right onto Llandudno Road (the Ship Inn opposite) and if you wish, enter the churchyard of St Trillo by the lych-gate. There are several seats here and good views. Cross the road to continue in the same direction but when you see a filling station across the road look for a footpath on your left. This will lead you into Stuart Drive and to the junction with Tan-y-bryn Road where you turn right. When you reach Rhos Road on the left, turn right onto a rough track.

Go up the steps on the right and follow the footpath to the remains of Llys Euryn (3). The path continues around the lip of a quarry (fenced off) and comes to a garage where you turn right. On the open hill look for a stone marker – no. 4 – and go left on a path through some trees until you are able to go up to the open ground above. This is somewhat steeper and leads to an OS trig point and a panorama table showing the hills of Snowdonia, their heights and distance from you. There are also the remains of a hill fort, (4) while the whole area is a nature reserve (5).

Retrace your steps to Tan-y-bryn Road, cross and go down Rhos Road which leads straight back to the Information Centre.

Should you wish just to climb Bryn Euryn you will find a little car park at GR 834802, a short way along the rough track. From there simply walk back to the steps to pick up the route.

Points of Interest:

(1) An inscription reads:

Parish of Llandrillo-yn-Rhos.
All reverence is due to this sacred spot.
This ancient chapel
is built over the holy well of St Trillo,
a Celtic Saint of the sixth century.
Pilgrim turn in and offer prayer.
The Lord be with you.

However as is sadly often the case nowadays, the chapel is usually locked and if you want to be sure of entry you must come to Mass which is celebrated on Fridays at 8.00 am.

(2) The inscription cannot be read from the road. It reads:

Prince Madog sailed from here
Aber-Kerrick-Gwynan, 1170 A.D.
and landed at Mobile Alabama
with his ships
Gorn Gwynant and Pedr Sant.

The story appeared in the writings of the antiquarian Humphrey Lluyd (see walk 6) and in the 16th century John Dee, a London Welshman, claimed that the Welsh had a title to the possession of America by virtue of Madog's voyages. Certainly by the 18th century stories circulated that there existed a Welsh-speaking tribe of Indians, the Madogwys. Reading an account of the voyage led John Evans of Waunfawr to explore and map the entire course of the Missouri in search of the tribe and, no doubt aided by widespread poverty, it also led to large scale migration from Wales to America.

Madog was the son of Owain Gwynedd, Madog ab Owain to give him his full name. Owain was an historical figure who died in December 1169 leaving nineteen sons and a civil war between two of them, Hywel and Dafydd, over the succession. Madog was an adventurous man less interested in the civil war than in a project to discover what lay beyond Ireland.

He prepared his ship, the Gwenan Gorn, built of oak planks joined by rivets of stags' horns and sailed from the harbour at the mouth of the Afon Ganol, now just those two pools in the garden of Odstone. The port was called Abercerrig-gwynion. His brother Rhiryd joined him at Lundy Island and they sailed west, nothing being heard of them for several years. When the ship returned it was a skeleton crew, the rest having stayed behind in the new land that Madog had discovered beyond the western horizon. Madog found enough men and women to fill ten ships and then set off never to be heard of again until rumours of the white-skinned, Welsh speaking tribe reached Europe.

In 1953, on the spot where it was supposed he landed, a memorial was raised by the Daughters of the American Revolution. It reads:

In memory of Prince Madog, A Welsh explorer,
who landed on the shores of Mobile Bay in 1170
and left behind, with the Indians, the Welsh language.

Despite the confident note of the inscription, and in the face of the inspiration given to the English poet Southey in his poem 'Madoc', and to a number of Welsh poets, the truth of the matter still remains to be resolved.

(3) Llys Euryn is a mediaeval hall now under the care of CADW, the Welsh Historic Monuments Agency, and currently being made safe. You can judge the size of the hall by the massive fireplace and chimney which are still standing.

(3) The outlines of the iron age hill fort are not easy to trace on the ground but any defensive position on this hill must have been difficult to assault. See Walk 9 for further notes on hill forts.

(4) The hill itself being limestone, the nature reserve contains many plants which flourish in that habitat including rock rose and scabious. The most notable is traveller's joy, a rarity in North Wales. Ask at the Information Centre for a guide.

Rhyl – James, the master mason

OS Map No.:	116
Start:	G.R. 014803. Car park at the Brickfield Pond on a minor road from the roundabout by the Crowned Bard Inn on the A525.
Access:	Rhyl is on the A548 coast road. Railway – Chester/Holyhead. Good bus connections.
Facilities:	All available in the town and in Rhuddlan, halfway round the walk.

Amount of climbing: Negligible.

The highlight of the walk is Rhuddlan Castle (1) built by James of St George (2) under the direction of Edward I. In the right conditions there are wildfowl and waders in abundance on the river.

Walk Directions: (-) denotes Point of Interest

Go out of the car park and turn right. In a few yards turn right again at a footpath sign by a playing field. The actual path is blocked but you can easily walk along the edge of the field instead. Cross a stile which is well hidden in the corner and go across the next field in the same direction to a gate and follow the fence on your left. This turns left to a bridge and a lane. Turn right onto the lane and when after 300m/330 yards it turns right at a farm, turn left on a stony track, which is a bridleway. When this turns left after 500m/550 yards you will see in a field on the right a small building – a gas pumping station. Cross one of the gates here and go along the left hand edge of the field past a gate on the left to a gate facing you. This gate is padlocked and there is no stile so climb it with care and turn right to another on the river bank (the Afon Clwyd). Turn left and stay on the embankment which takes you under the Rhuddlan bypass. When your way is blocked leave the embankment, descend to the lane now alongside, go up to the main

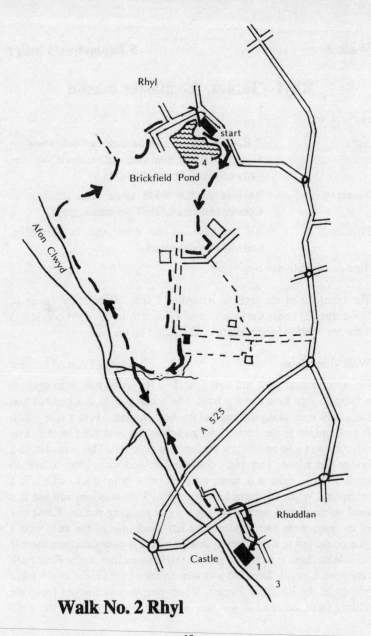

Rhyl

start

Brickfield Pond

4

Afon Clwyd

A 525

Rhuddlan

Castle

1

3

Walk No. 2 Rhyl

road and turn left. The castle is signposted along the first turning to the right. Having visited the castle return to the main road and turn right if you wish to see the Parliament Building or find one of the little cafés.

Retrace your steps to the river embankment. If you are interested in wild flowers you will find a better selection on the salt flats down to your left. From the bypass it is about 2km/1¼ miles before the path turns right with a high wire fence alongside. Cross a farm track with a gate in the fence and continue until you reach a signpost indicating the Brickfield Pond (4) to the right. Go in this direction round the back of a caravan park to a road. Turn left and in about 400m/¼ mile you will find a gate on the right. Go through this and turn left onto a path leading back to the car park.

Points of Interest:

(1) In mid July 1277 King Edward I moved his army from Chester to Flint at the beginning of his offensive to put down the uprising of Llywelyn ap Gruffudd. Here he began the construction of the castle still standing today but by August Edward had moved his forward base to Rhuddlan where there had already been a Norman earth and timber castle (3). Work began almost at once and the basic structure of the castle was virtually complete by the autumn of 1280.

In addition, the river was deepened by hand to enable supplies to be brought directly from the sea. At Flint 2,300 diggers had been recruited to work on the castle and they gradually moved across to Rhuddlan. Among them were 300 who had been marched from Lincolnshire guarded by three sergeants on horseback. It may be supposed that they were unwilling recruits who were bringing their experience of building dykes in the fenland around Boston.

As you will see, three sides of the castle had a moat, the fourth sloping down to the river. The outer wall was low so that arrows could be fired from the inner ward over the outer ranks of bowmen. The inner ward is a diamond shape with two gatehouses and two towers.

It is difficult for us to imagine what the castle was like when occupied since the wooden buildings where people actually lived have decayed. We can still see, though, holes where floor beams were fitted into the walls, and the marks where the roofline used to be. It is recorded that there was a King's Hall with a painted chamber; a Queen's Hall; kitchens and a chapel. In the outer ward were stables, granaries, a forge and so on. Queen Eleanor was particularly fond of Rhuddlan and the account books reveal that she had a fishpond constructed with seats round it and had the courtyard turfed.

As Edward moved further westward he continued to build his great chain of castles – Conwy, Harlech, Caernarfon, Beaumaris – and the strategic importance of Rhuddlan lessened. Its historic importance is that it was here on 19 March 1284 that the Rhuddlan Statute was proclaimed. The Statute, enforced and much hated, claimed to give the Welsh in the north 'judicial rights and independence'. It was, in effect, the law by which they were to be ruled, and remained in force until the Act of Union in 1536. On the main street is a stone building known as the Parliament House, which has on its wall a tablet commemorating the Statute.

Rhuddlan shared the fate of many ancient castles in the Civil War. Artillery proved too much for the walls and there was no reason to rebuild it.

(2) In 1296 Master James of St George wrote, ' . . . as you know, Welshmen are Welshmen, and you need to understand them properly'. In 1277, however, he was just beginning to acquire that understanding with the construction of Rhuddlan castle.

He is first mentioned in 1261 when he was working on the castle of Yverdon in Savoy and took his name from his work on the castle of St Georges d'Esperanche which Edward saw on his return from a crusade in 1273. Five years later he was taken into the king's service specifically to design and construct castles to hold down the Welsh. He was responsible entirely or largely for 12 of the castles in Wales and went on to be appointed constable of Harlech Castle for three years, an unusual post for a man who was not Norman and not of the nobility. He later built castles in Scotland and died about 1309 as life tenant of Mostyn manor in Flintshire.

(3) The site of the old castle is to the south of Edward's and is reached by a bridge over the now dry moat. Twthill, as it is known, was built in

1073 by Robert of Rhuddlan and his cousin the Earl of Chester, called Hugh the Fat. The two used the castle as a base for their many ruthless attacks on the Welsh, mainly along the coast. The castle was taken at least three times by the Welsh and recaptured by the English over the next 200 years before Edward made it redundant.

It is now little more than a mound, its defensive ditch silted up and its wooden tower decayed. There is some indication that it might have been rebuilt in stone and just to the north you can see the outlines of the outer walls or bailey.

(4) The clay subsoil provided the raw materials for four factories producing the bricks from which Edwardian Rhyl was built. 'Blaster Bates' demolished the 200' high chimney in 1978 and fifteen years later work began to create the wildlife haven that you see today.

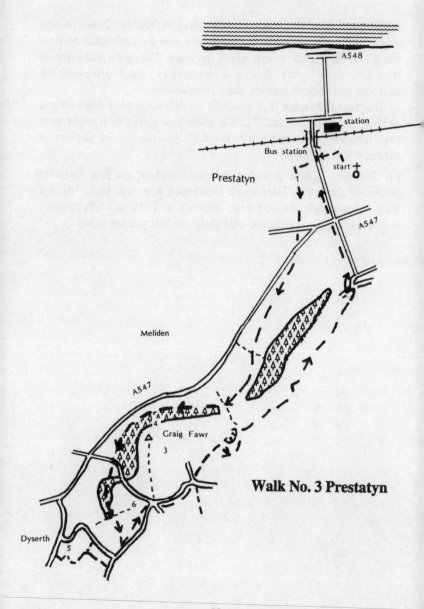

A548

station

Bus station

start

Prestatyn

1

A547

A547

Meliden

Graig Fawr

3

4

6

Dyserth

5

Walk No. 3 Prestatyn

Prestatyn – behind the sea-side

OS Map No.:	116
Start:	G.R. 067828. Behind the library and council offices.
Access:	Prestatyn is on the A548 coast road and has good rail and bus connections.
Facilities:	Full range in the town and in Dyserth.
Amount of climbing:	180m/600ft.

Rhuddlan Borough Council has converted an old railway track (1) into what is now called the Prestatyn/Dyserth Walkway which formerly linked areas of intense industrial activity (2). The route follows the Walkway and then joins up with Offa's Dyke Path. Two extensions are suggested: a visit to the village of Dyserth with its waterfall, and an ascent of Graig Fawr (3). The outward route is very easy with pleasant views but the return is quite spectacular with much of Snowdonia and many of the hills of mid Wales on view, while the Lancashire coast with Formby Point is also visible. The hillsides are rich in plants, including lots of orchids but it is the dense masses of gorse which will linger in the memory.

Walk Directions: (-) denotes Point of Interest

The most difficult part of the navigation on this walk is finding the start! Use the long stay car park on the east side of the High Street (one way traffic). Walk back to the High Street by Nant Hall Road, cross and turn left. Take the first on the right, Kings Road, which passes the Post Office. You will pass the clinic and come to the WRVS building on the corner. Half left over the main road is Banastre Avenue which you can safely reach by using the pelican crossing. At the far end of this short avenue turn left as signposted onto the Walkway, just by the car park of the surgery.

Stay on this track for about 4km/2½ miles. You will pass a golf course, after which the track curves left under the cliffs (4) of Graig Fawr, passing through cuttings and heavily wooded on the left. Only when you see an open field on the left do you have to think about leaving the track. The track passes over a bridge and in 200m/220 yards goes under a stone bridge with a brick arch. At this point go left to the lane above and turn right. There is a conveniently sited bench a short distance to the left if you wish to have a break here.

(To visit Dyserth turn left to the bench, which is at a T junction and turn right 20m/22 yards further on over a signposted stile. The enclosed path leads to another stile and a grassy field. Keep straight on towards a little rise in the ground with hawthorn trees and soon you will see a low post with a waymarker. Go downhill with the trees on our right onto a path through the wood. Just below this you meet a track at a T junction. Turn left, over the stile, and follow the path which leads over a stream and up to a lane. Turn immediately right and go down some steps past a bungalow called 'Lapwing'. Steps lead down to the village street where you turn right for the waterfall (5), café, pubs and toilets. To continue the walk retrace your steps to the bridge over the track. The extension is an extra 1km/½ mile and 60m/200'.)

Follow the lane uphill to a T junction, turn left and at the junction a few yards on, turn right (6).

(To extend the walk over Graig Fawr go through the gate at the back of the National Trust car park which you can see across the road. A thin path leads up to the concrete triangulation pillar on the summit. Retrace your steps to the car park and turn left to follow the main route. This extension adds about 1km/½ mile and 55m/180'.)

Turn left at the junction by Laburnum Cottage and then right, through a gate with the words 'Red Roofs'. Go through the gate immediately to the right of this property. Your route is now adequately signposted as befits a National Trail. The waymarkers that you follow are the yellow arrow (public footpath) accompanied by a white acorn (National Trail – in this case, Offa's Dyke).

The path goes round the lip of a disused quarry before taking a right fork signposted 'Prestatyn' and a left signposted 'Bryn Prestatyn'. The next signpost 'Prestatyn' points to the right and uphill. This next section is quite steep but it does not last long – just take your time. Follow the white acorns and ignore another footpath over a stile to the right.

The path now begins to descend towards the town, the way made easier by a series of wooden steps. When you reach a road, turn left still following the acorns which you will find all the way through the streets. The road curves right, reaches a junction where you turn right then bends left. Go over a crossroads into the High Street and turn right into Nant Hall road again for the car park.

Points of Interest:

(1) The railway was opened as a goods line in 1869 by the London & North Western Railway Co. It was built to serve the villages of Meliden and Dyserth which lie under a limestone escarpment from which not only was limestone quarried but veins of minerals including lead, zinc and silver had been mined since Roman times. In 1905 the line was opened to passenger traffic as a result of a public campaign but by 1930 had reverted to goods traffic as road transport developed. The line closed in 1973, its last business with Dyserth quarry which lasted only another eight years.

The stations were small halts which have now disappeared as there were no substantial structures such as platforms. Instead, the carriages had folding steps but this meant that the platform at Prestatyn was unsuitable and a small gravelled area at the end of the platform was used instead. The original trains were railmotors, a carriage with a steam engine in a compartment at one end although these were replaced by normal rolling stock at a later date.

(2) All along the track is evidence of this activity: overgrown quarries, spoil heaps, limekilns, leats to carry water, ore chutes, buildings of many sorts, shafts and the openings of horizontal 'levels'.

(3) Graig Fawr, while not the highest point of the walk, offers good views towards Snowdonia and to sea. It is a designated conservation

area bequeathed to the National Trust by Sir Geoffrey Summers of the John Summers Steelworks at Shotton. In the words of the Trust the 'limestone hill supports an outstanding variety of flowers and butterflies'. Rock Rose, food plant of the Brown Argus butterfly can be found. Bishopswood, a little further on in the walk, belongs to the local council and is a Site of Special Scientific Interest. The pedunculate oak, a type rare in Wales, flourishes on the boulder clay overlying the limestone at this point. Among rare flowers is Ffynnon Fair on Mary's Well.

(4) The cliff is the fossilised remains of a coral reef. This would have been laid down as the remains of coral and the shells of dead sea creatures about 340 million years ago and was originally much further south than it is now.

When rocks were pushed upwards by pressure from within the earth to form mountain chains, cracks developed in the limestone which were filled with molten minerals like lead, silver and zinc.

Softer rocks were laid down over the limestone but with time they eroded, exposing the limestone and during the Ice Ages glaciers carved out the Vale of Clwyd, leaving behind layers of boulder clay. As the limestone now formed a cliff rising above this valley, the horizontal and vertical cracks containing the valuable minerals became relatively easy to exploit.

(5) Dyserth Falls had a reputation for healing properties and were consequently visited for that reason. They remain popular as a tourist attraction with their drop of some 60 feet. There is a small entry fee.

(6) Just below this point is the site of Dyserth Castle built by Henry III in 1241 and destroyed by Llywelyn ap Gruffudd in 1263. Centuries of quarrying have left little to see.

St Asaph – the survival of the Welsh language

OS Map No.:	116
Start:	G.R. 039743 (Cathedral) or 036743 (bridge).
Access:	St Asaph is bypassed by the A55 trunk road and is on the 51/52/53 bus service from Rhyl to Corwen.
Facilities:	Toilets in riverside car park; several pubs and restaurants; Farm Shop and Turners cafés.

Amount of climbing: 25m/80ft.

This is an easy stroll based around the river Clwyd, giving you the opportunity to visit the smallest cathedral in Britain (1) one of whose incumbents played a crucial role in ensuring the survival of the Welsh language (2).

Walk Directions: (-) denotes Point of Interest

Come out of the Cathedral car park and turn left. Go over the pedestrian crossing into Mount Road whcih soon curves right past Fairholme Prep School and then left where there is a sign saying 'Weak Bridge'. Cross the A55 Expressway and keep on this lane which passes Pen y Bryn farm and continues between hedges. To the right are pleasant views of the northern end of the Clwydian range including the village of Dyserth below Graig Fawr (see Walk no. 3) and to the left the spire of the marble church at Bodelwyddan.

Cross the signposted stile on the right by a green metal bench and turn left along the side of the field. Pass into the next field and then very quickly into the next. Go half right to the right hand side of the field. Do not cross onto the disused railway line but keep to the right edge of the field which becomes gradually narrower and ends at a stile.

Cross and continue towards Pentre farm. Go through a wooden gate on the right and then through two metal gates to pass between the

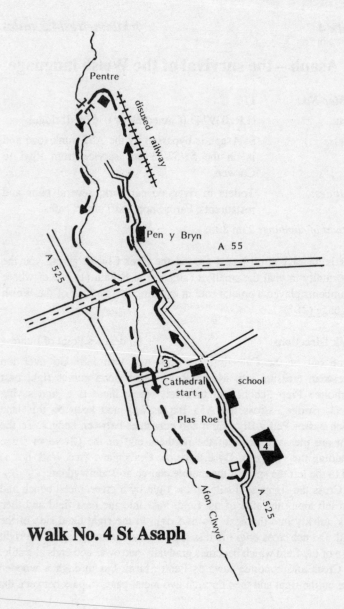

Pentre

disused railway

Pen y Bryn

A 55

A 525

3

Cathedral start 1

school

Plas Roe

4

Afon Clwyd

A 525

Walk No. 4 St Asaph

outbuildings onto the farm road. Turn left and follow it to a T junction almost opposite some steps leading to a bridge over the River Clwyd. Cross the river, turn left and in fifty yards go up steps on the right which lead to a stile and the embankment.

Walk south with the river down on your left for about 880m/½ mile until you reach a lane. Cross this ignoring the river bridge and continue on the riverside, now with bungalows on the right. The path goes beneath the A55 and passes first the livestock market and then the Fire Station. The path drops from the embankment for a short distance but about 90m/100 yards before a stone road bridge watch for the chance to climb onto the embankment again. Cross to the road by some houses to the main road. Turn left and cross to the pedestrian bridge. If you wish you can continue up the hill straight back to the Cathedral car park visiting the Parish Church (3) behind the main street to the left.

To continue the walk turn to the right just before the Fountain Garage into Plas Roe public park. From here there is a choice of paths all going south, including one by the riverbank which I shall describe. After 400m/¼ mile cross a stile just past some tennis courts and continue until you are past the last of the houses which you can see on the high ground up to your left. Incline half left and you will find another stile. Cross this and go left up the embankment and to the right of a metal gate. In the corner of the field is a stile leading to a path enclosed by barbed wire. Cross a further stile and then go through the metal gate immediately on the right and follow the fence round to the left to reach a stile and footpath sign on the road. Turn left to reach the Cathedral car park passing on the right H.M. Stanley Hospital (4).

Points of Interest:

(1) The cathedral, the smallest in Britain and one of the oldest in Wales, has survived several attempts to move the see to other locations. The original church was founded in 560 by St Kentigern who entrusted it to his pupil, Asaph, when he returned to Glasgow. The building was restored in 1868-75 by Sir Gilbert Scott but since then has had much money spent on internal ornamentation which is not

to everybody's liking. This was not, however, the first re-building of the cathedral which was ravaged by the English Kings Henry III and Edward I before being burnt down by Owain Glyndŵr and finally being mis-used by Cromwell's forces in the civil war.

(2) In front of the Cathedral is a monument to a group of men who between them brought about one of the most remarkable episodes in Welsh history, by laying the foundations by which the Welsh language was able to survive into the 20th century. Where other Celtic languages like Cornish now have no native speakers, and others like Gaelic have a tenuous existence, Welsh is more vigorous than ever. It had to withstand though, the deliberate attempts of English monarchs and governments to suppress it; to resist the natural tendency of those who wished to better themselves by preferring English to their mother tongue; and to be inventive enough to stand up against the economic and political power conferred upon speakers of English, now more than ever a world language.

In the Act of Union in 1536 Henry VIII outlawed Welsh for anybody who wished to hold public office but by 1563 Elizabeth I passed an act allowing the translation of the Bible into Welsh 'because the English tongue is not understood of the most and greatest number of all her majesty's most loving and obedient servants inhabiting . . . Wales' – testimony to the strength of the language and a measure probably invoked by fear of Catholicism.

William Morgan, Bishop of St Asaph, was responsible for the translation which was published in 1588 and became the standard for written Welsh and in many places the sole means of its survival. When, for example, the industrial revolution brought English workers, mine owners and entrepreneurs into Wales they brought with them their language. Welsh remained the language of the chapel, though and up to the middle of the 19th century most of the populace were Welsh speaking even though there was official discouragement.

One method which I have personally always found distressing to think about ever since it was first described to me was used in schools. A piece of wood with the words 'Welsh Not' was hung around the neck of the first pupil heard speaking Welsh each day. That pupil was allowed to pass it on to another Welsh speaker and the unfortunate pupil wearing it when school ended was thrashed.

From 90% Welsh speakers in 1851 there was a steady decline to 19% in 1981. Since then there has been an increase, particularly among young people and Welsh seems to be in a strong position. Campaigns by the Welsh language society, Cymdeithas yr Iaith Gymraeg, have led to simple things that we can all see, like road signs in two languages. There are others that the outsider will be unaware of like the right to conduct all your affairs, tax included, in your mother tongue or the growth of Welsh language classes, film, TV pop, literature, children's books and above all the facility to be educated in Welsh from nursery to university.

Look at the monument and think about it.

(3) The parish church contains the graves of two noteworthy men. Siôn Tudur had been a member of the 'band of tall personable men' who were the bodyguard of Elizabeth I, herself a Welsh speaker. He retired to St Asaph at about the age of fifty, describing himself as an old poet, 'hen fardd', when Dr Morgan's Bible was published. Although I cannot speak from personal knowledge, his writings are said to be noted for 'simplicity, unusual directness and clear expression of his thoughts.'

The second is Dic Aberdaron or Richard Jones who lived here only for the last few months of his life. He died in 1843 aged 63 after a lifetime wandering through Wales and England. He was noted for his skills as a linguist, being fluent in Welsh, English, Latin, Hebrew, Greek, French, Spanish and Italian. He apparently had knowledge of others like Arabic and the ancient languages of Syria and Chaldea and produced a Welsh/Greek/Hebrew dictionary which is in the Cathedral Museum. He was always poor and depended upon patrons to keep himself. This may explain why he went barefoot and had a ragged appearance, always carrying many books and usually a harp through the streets of Liverpool where he spent many years. On his gravestone is a verse in Welsh which has been translated:

A linguist eightfold above linguists.
A man who was a dictionary of all regions.

Death took his fifteen languages away.
Now he lies below with no language at all.

(4) The hospital was formerly the 'Union Workhouse' but has been re-named after H.M. Stanley born John Rowlands in Ruthin (see Walk no. 8). It was from here that he ran away to sea in 1856 after being maltreated at the hands of the Workhouse teacher, James Francis.

(5) The North Wales International Music Festival, held in the Cathedral in late September each year, is associated with the Welsh composer William Mathias who was its Artistic Director from 1972. He was Professor of Music at Bangor from 1970 to 1988 and a composer in many modes, including three symphonies, church, choral, chamber and organ music. In 1997 top price tickets were for the BBC National Orchestra of Wales at £14. With many other performances at £4 it is a relatively low-cost venue for lovers of classical music and with careful planning could be combined with walking to make a pleasant late holiday.

Holywell – saints and slavery

OS Map No.:   116

Start: G.R. 194774. Greenfield Valley car park on the
                     B5121.

Access: The car park can be reached from the A548 or by
                     leaving the A55 at the Holywell turn-off.
                     Chester/Rhyl buses.

Facilities: Near the car park are toilets, information centre
                     and a café; at St Winifred's Well, religious
                     souvenirs and toilets; by Holywell bus station, a
                     café.

Amount of climbing: 70m/220ft.

This is a walk full of interest, including industrial archaeology, legend
and an abbey. It is also in a very pretty, wooded area with expanses of
water, the source of power for the mills. There is a farm with buildings
brought from other parts of North Wales, and an adventure
playground. The walk is almost entirely on well-made tracks.

Walk Directions: (-) denotes Point of Interest

From the car park (1) follow the only path (which is signposted). This
takes you past a building on your right. Follow the building around
two corners and pass the Environmental Centre noting on your left the
wooden statue. Ahead now is a garden with bandstand on the site of
the Abbey Mill (2). The route continues on the tarmac lane to the left.
Steps on the right give access to the site of the Lower Cotton Mill (3).
Fork right from the tarmac lane to keep by the side of the millpool.
Fork left to go up four wooden steps. At the junction of two major
paths, steps on the right lead down to the site of Meadow Mill (4) and
its pool. Take the right fork.

Two unsignposted paths on the right give access to the chimney

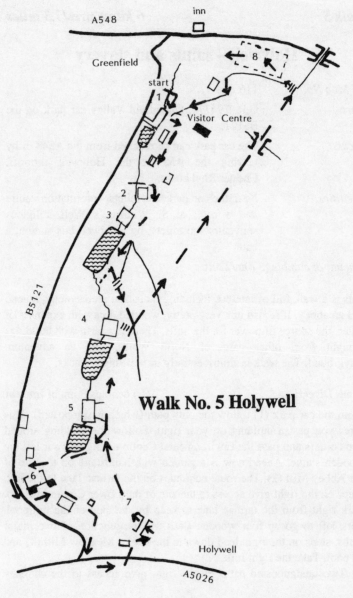

A548

inn

Greenfield

start

1

Visitor Centre

2

3

B5121

4

Walk No. 5 Holywell

5

6

7

Holywell

A5026

and other remains of the Battery Works (5). Just past the second of these take the right fork signposted to Holywell. Pass through an iron gate, down past some factory buildings to the road and turn left. (The Royal Oak is to the right.) St Winifred's Well (6) is 100m/110 yards further on. (20p admission, toilets). Leave the Chapel and turn left to continue uphill.

Turn left, through a pair of iron gates by the church, and continue uphill by the white railings. The road takes you past Plas Dewi and the Beaufort Arms to the junction with the main road where you turn left.

Go through the car park on the left to pass Delyn Press Printers. Do not cross the bridge in front of you but go down the concrete ramp on the right and turn left to pass underneath the bridge onto the old railway track (7).

Stay on this track which shortly joins your outward route. Ignore turnings to the left and keep straight ahead at two major crossings. You eventually cross a bridge and soon some steps on the left lead to Basingwerk Abbey (8) and beyond it all the facilities of the Heritage Park including the car park.

Points of Interest:

(1) The car park is the first of the industrial sites and like the majority in the valley was a copper works. Each had its own speciality and most belonged to the Parys Mine Company. Here were rolled sheets of copper to make cladding for wooden hulled ships to give protection against parasites that attacked them in the tropics. The Parys copper mines are on Anglesey and date back to Roman times. It was, however, only in 1768 that the 'Great Lode' was struck, making it the most productive mine in Europe.

(2) These ruins, now a garden, are of the Abbey Mill specialising in copper and brass wire for making nails and pins.

(3) The restored building here was the warehouse of the Lower Cotton Mill, built in ten weeks in 1785. The world famous Thomas Pennant, born nearby, watched its six storeys rise 'like the Tower of Babel'. In its later life it was used to grind corn.

(4) Meadow Mill produced copper rollers for printing cloth.

(5) The ruins of the Battery Works have some of the most poignant history of all in the valley. Brass sheets were stamped out to make pots and pans which were exported through Liverpool to Africa. The goods were used as payment for slaves who were taken to America to work on the cotton fields. The cotton was then brought back for processing so that the ships always had a full cargo. Also in demand were brass and copper rods which could be fashioned into rings or ornaments or used as currency. The buildings burnt down in the 1950's after being used for the manufacture of clothing.

(6) St Winifred's Well, the holy well which gave its name to the town, is within a 16th century chapel. The waters were used medicinally by the Romans but the legend of the Well began in 660 AD when a Prince Caradoc tried to seduce the beautiful Gwenffrewi or Winifred. When she refused and escaped, Caradoc pursued her and cut off her head. Her uncle, St Beuno, reunited her head with her body, placed a curse upon the descendants of Caradoc and caused Caradoc himself to melt into the ground. A white scar remained around her neck and water gushed from the ground where her head had fallen. The shrine became one of the great places of pilgrimage in the Christian world and immersion in the well is believed to have powers of healing. Among its many notable visitors was Henry V who came here before his attack on France which ended with the battle of Agincourt. The story of the removal of St Winifred's body to Shrewsbury Abbey is the basis of the first Brother Cadfael story 'A Morbid Taste for Bones' by Ellis Peters.

(7) The path here is on the trackbed of a standard gauge railway that closed in 1954. Originally built as a mineral line it changed to passenger use and has carried many thousands of pilgrims to St Winifred's Well.

(8) Basingwerk Abbey dates from 1131. The monks were of the Cistercian order (White monks, from the colour of their clothing). They used the power of the stream to grind corn and they also mined lead and silver. The Abbey was very rich and powerful, being patronised by both Welsh and English princes. For instance, the monks were granted the manor of Glossop in Derbyshire and also owned Llyn Tegid (Bala Lake) and grazing rights in that area. After the

monasteries were dissolved in 1536 stone and fittings were taken to other churches in Wales. Later, many of the stones were used to build the mills in the valley.

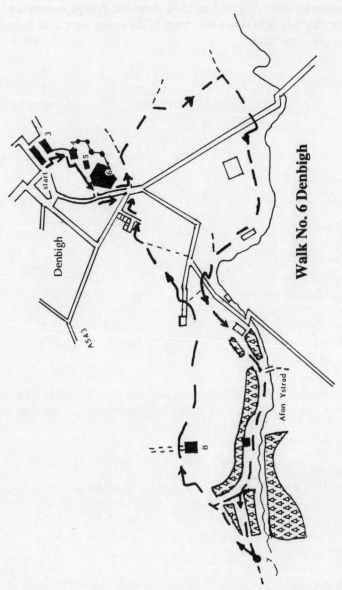

Walk No. 6 Denbigh

Denbigh

A543

start

Afon Ystrad

38

Denbigh – castles and characters

OS Map No.:   116

Start: G.R. 053661. The library/information centre in the High Street.

Access: Denbigh is on the A525, south of St Asaph. Bus service No. 51/52/53 service from Rhyl, and No. A50/A52 from Holywell.

Facilities: There are many cafés and pubs in the town. Public toilets are signposted.

Amount of climbing: 50m/175ft.

Denbigh (1) is another of the charming towns of Dyffryn Clwyd with much historical and architectural interest. Several personages (2) important in Welsh, English and, indeed, international history are associated with the town. The walk itself takes us to a literary oddity as an excuse to sample the valley of the Afon Ystrad and take in some outstanding landscapes.

Walk Directions: (-) denotes Point of Interest

Face the library entrance and take the road to the right of it. Turn right up Bull Lane just before the Bull Inn (3) which you can see almost as you start. The road goes uphill, turns right and then left again and passes the ruins of Leicester's Church (4) and then the tower of St Hilary's Church (5). In front of you, at the top of the hill, is Denbigh Castle (6). If you are visiting the castle, turn left when you come out. Otherwise continue past the castle on a road which descends, with the castle on your left.

At a T junction there is a black and white, half-timbered building, Castell Lodge. Turn left and in about 45m/50 yards turn left again on a signposted stony track which descends under a canopy of trees. Turn to the right through a kissing gate and walk with the hedge on your right to the next kissing gate where a signpost directs you half left across the field.

In front of you is a small gate and on your right a stile. Cross the stile and walk with the hedge on your left to a kissing gate and at the end of the next field, two farm gates. Go through the right hand gate and continue with the hedge now on your right to a stile and then to another on the right. This leads to a path between hedges and over two more stiles to a lane.

Turn right here and shortly turn left onto a rough track where a wall begins. The track ends at a house on your right but continues as a path leading to a metal gate. Keep ahead with the river over to your left and following a fence. When a track joins from the right descend slightly to a stile and maintain direction. The path goes through a clearing where you can see a white house above you to the right. Just before another white cottage (at your level) go half right to a stile on a lane.

Turn to the right on the lane and double back onto the first signposted path on the left. Stay on this path which eventually passes a garden wall on your left. Keep ahead on the path and do not cross the footbridge which you come to on your left. Pass through two metal gates with stiles. A ruinous cottage on the right mostly hidden by trees is the cottage where Dr Johnson used to stay.

The track divides after the second gate. Do not go up the steep path but keep on the level one which leads out of the wood by a gate. Dr Johnson's Monument (7) is down to the left by the river. After viewing the monument return to the gate and continue up the hill with the wood on your right passing a stile and gate in the corner. Keep the wood on your right, and just over the top of the hill go through a gate with a stile. Turn left, go through another gate with a stone stile and in 18m/20 yards turn right, over another stile. Follow the high brick wall on your right to a stile and gate and then cross the driveway of the large house, Gwaenynog (8).

Continue on a track through a gate with a smaller wooden gate by it. The track continues to two more gateways (not the one half left though). Now descend, the hedge on your left, to a stile by a Tudor cottage whose white chimney will be seen first. Continue onto a lane and in 45m/50 yards cross a stone stile on the left. Go half right over the field to a gateway and stone stile and with the hedge on your right walk towards some bungalows. A stile and enclosed path lead to a road.

Turn left and then right at the junction to reach Castell Lodge and your outward route.

Points of Interest:

(1) Dinbych, anglicised to Denbigh, is the Welsh name of the town and means 'little fort'. When the river Clwyd formed the boundary with England, the crossing was defended by a castle built by Dafydd, brother of Llywelyn ap Gruffudd. Although it seems reasonable to suppose that this was the origin of the town's name, there is a much more interesting, if less plausible, explanation. John Salusbury, a mediaeval knight, was believed to have magical powers because he had two thumbs and was therefore called Siôn Bodiau. When a dragon occupied the castle and terrorised the town it was Siôn who returned with the dragon's head calling in triumph, 'Dim Bych' – no dragon – which was corrupted into Dinbych. Siôn had taken advantage of the dragon, it seems, while it was counting his thumbs!

(2) Close by the castle was a cottage in which was born one John Rowlands and if you have never heard his name you certainly know the understatement for which he became famous – 'Dr Livingstone, I presume'. Rowlands was sent as an orphan to the workhouse in St Asaph but ran away to sea, changed his name to Henry Morton Stanley and joined the staff of the New York Herald. He made his scoop when he was sent to search for Livingstone who had not been heard from for some years. Another local person who changed his name but is not known to many non-Welsh speakers was Thomas Edwards. He was born in 1739 about 13km/8 miles to the north-west of Denbigh on a farm near Llannefydd and is buried in St Marcella's Church on the outskirts of Denbigh. He is better known as Twm o'r Nant and was the eldest of ten children. He worked on the farm but by

the age of nine had already begun to write poetry, a remarkable accomplishment at a time when illiteracy was almost universal, in England at least. He wrote interludes, a kind of folk play in rhyme, and toured Wales with them performing from a farm cart at fairs. Their success was due to the fact that they were rooted in the reality of his own life and they are still recognised as a valuable insight into the life of the poor at that time.

An antiquary, Humphrey Llwyd (1527-68) was also a native of the town. He studied medicine at Oxford and after service as a private physician to a noble family returned home. He published a calendar from which the phases of the moon could be calculated – for ever – and the first separate map of Wales.

Well known to Welsh speakers and patriots is the name of Thomas Gee, a local printer and publisher, who in the 19th century brought out *Baner ac Amserau Cymru* (The Banner and Welsh Times). This is still published and it had a great influence on public opinion in Wales in Gee's lifetime.

From the same parish as Twm o'r Nant came Catrin o Ferain, known as Mam Cymru, the Mother of Wales, because through four marriages so many leading Welsh families could trace their ancestry to her. Her second husband proposed to her on the way to the funeral of the first and her third on the way back. Those marriages took place in due course, followed by another. Four Weddings and a Funeral doesn't come into it.

(3) A newel post in the form of a glove in the Bull Inn reminds us of one the traditional industries of Denbigh – glovemaking. Sir Richard Clough, Catrin's second husband was the son of a glove maker and he later became a merchant.

(4) In 1563 Robert Dudley, Earl of Leicester and the favourite of Queen Elizabeth I, was granted the Lordship of Denbigh and proceeded on the construction of the only large church of the period in Britain. It was reputed to be a replacement for St Asaph Cathedral but it was never completed and became known as Leicester's Folly.

(5) St Hilary's Tower is all that remains of the garrison church.

Because of the rock there was never a graveyard here. Another important building in the town, although not on our route, is the Friary established in 1289. It was relatively intact until a fire in 1898.

(6) I find Denbigh Castle to be one of the finest in the area to visit despite its ruinous condition compared say with Conwy or Caernarfon. This is probably because of its position on this commanding hilltop thought to be the site of the stronghold of Dafydd (see (1) above). After Dafydd's attack on Hawarden Castle in March 1282, Edward I systematically annihilated all opposition but Denbigh castle held out for almost a month, falling in October of the same year. Edward granted the Lordship to Henry de Lacy and the present castle was planned by James of St George (see Walk no. 2) although de Lacy continued the work later from his own resources.

By 1284 he began to stock a deer park and in 1290 he granted the town a borough charter, but this benefited only the English settlers who were brought in. The half finished castle obviously became a prime target for the Welsh who attacked and captured it under Madog ap Llewelyn in 1294, holding it for a year. The construction continued (in a different coloured stone) but the castle was incomplete when de Lacy died in 1311. The historian John Leland, writing in 1535, tells us that de Lacy lost interest in the work after his eldest son was drowned in the well.

During the early years of the Glyndŵr uprisings, the castle was held by Hotspur (Henry Percy), who later came to support Owain Glyndŵr. It was held by the Yorkists in the Wars of the Roses and by the Royalists under Colonel William Salesbury of Rûg, in the Civil War. King Charles I spent three days here in 1645, but the castle was captured in the following year after a siege of six months. As was usual, Cromwell's forces destroyed the castle's defences, making it redundant.

(7) Dr Johnson's Monument is the literary oddity I mentioned, a strangely urban feature to find in a remote field by a river. It was erected by his host to commemorate visits by the doctor to Gwaenynog in 1774 and looks very much like an urn to hold funeral ashes. Dr Johnson remarked caustically: 'Mr Myddleton's erection of an urn

looks like an intention to bury me alive. Let him think for the present of some more acceptable memorial'. The doctor had visited in the company of his close friend Mrs Thrale, only child of John Salusbury (that name again) of Bachygraig. In 1786 she published her 'Anecdotes of the late Samuel Johnson' and in 1788 her correspondence with him. Dr Johnson is probably not known as widely as he was, although you may recall Robbie Coltrane playing him in a TV dramatisation of Boswell's *Journal of a Tour to the Hebrides*. He lived from 1709 to 1784 and was the centre of London literary life, a wit, critic, journalist, novelist and dramatist. Perhaps his greatest achievement was his compilation of one of the earliest dictionaries of the English language, not quite the first but certainly the finest.

(8) Gwaenynog was the home of the Myddleton family for five hundred years but was sold to the Burtons, Beatrix Potter's Uncle Fred. Beatrix loved the old house with its low-ceilinged rooms and she made many sketches of the old, traditionally carved Welsh furniture. The walled garden though, on the other side of the brick wall we walk past, made a particularly strong impression, and it formed the basis of the garden which Mr McGregor cultivated in 'The Tale of the Flopsy Bunnies'. 'It is,' she wrote, 'very productive but not tidy, the prettiest kind of garden, where bright old-fashioned flowers grow amongst the currant bushes.' She also writes about a picnic at Dr Johnson's Monument, when they were caught in a thunderstorm.

Nannerch – Arthur's resting place

OS Map No.:	116
Start:	G.R. 169689. A large lay-by at the turn-off to Nannerch.
Access:	Nannerch is 6.5 miles west of Mold on the A541. Bus no. 14, Mold/Denbigh (M&H).
Facilities:	There is a village pub and other pubs and cafés on the A541.

Amount of climbing: 305m/1000ft.

This is an attractive walk in the centre of the Clwydian Range Area of Outstanding Natural Beauty (AONB) (1). Good tracks make the gradual height gain very easy.

Walk Directions: (-) denotes Point of Interest

Begin by walking south along the A541 in the Mold direction for 300m/330 yards and turn right along a driveway immediately past the first house. After 250m/275 yards, the drive turns sharply right and you will soon see a white, sliding gate on the left. Go through this, through the garden and stay on this main track. Pass a left fork down to a house by a wood and go along an avenue of tall trees to an iron gate by a derelict cottage. The track only becomes vague when it goes through a meadow but beyond the gate ahead the route is clear again. The track has now a fence on the right but parts company with it at a gate and begins to curve SE, levelling out and becoming grassy again. Soon you will see on the left a low mound with a pile of stones, perhaps a cairn or the ruins of a barn. At this point leave the track and turn right to go uphill. A distinct, if small, path develops leading to a gate in a fence. Go through this and up to the summit of Moel Arthur (2).

Return to the gate and turn left following the fence at first along a

Walk No. 7 Nannerch

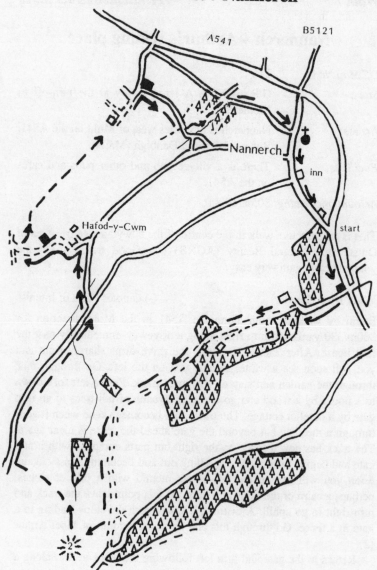

section of Offa's Dyke path with the white acorn marking a National Trail and the yellow arrow of a public footpath. Two stiles lead to a grassy slope where some care may be needed, and down to a lane where you turn right.

Follow the lane down until you come to a junction. Both branches bring you back to Nannerch but the lane ahead climbs a hill and carries more traffic and I prefer to turn left. Once in the village turn right for the car parking area.

A much better way back, however, adds only 2km/1.5 miles and 90m/300' to the walk. About 400m/¼ mile down the left turn, go left again into a narrow lane, pass the drive to Hafod-y-Cwm and soon turn up an unmarked, stony track on the right between hedges. This turns sharply left and goes past the front of a whitewashed cottage before passing under trees. When it is clear of the trees it joins another track coming in from the left. At this point leave the track and climb a gate on the right. This is an unsignposted footpath. An indistinct path leads half right (bearing 50°) across the field towards a clump of trees and a gate which you go through. Go uphill keeping close to the fence on your left. Cross a stile and follow a row of trees to the brow of the hill where there is a stile by a gate. It is worth pausing here to look back at the great hill fort of Penycloddiau and to its left Moel Arthur. From the gate keep on in the same direction (bearing 80°) to a stile over an electric fence and a further stile by a clump of trees. This is the start of an enclosed green lane leading down over stiles and past the front door of a cottage to a stony track and then a surfaced lane.

Keep on downhill for 45m/50 yards and take the turning on the right, going uphill with the farm buildings on your left. The lane goes down again and just past the first house on the right look for a stile on the left. This is below eye level and at some times of year may be obscured by vegetation. Once over it, go down to the signpost at the bottom of the field and turn left as indicated, following the line of a stream to a stile. This leads to a woodland track alongside the stream which comes out at a lane.

Turn right, ignore the lane on the left but go past the bench and uphill once more to the main street in Nannerch. Turn right for the car parking area.

Points of Interest:

(1) The area was designated as an AONB in 1985 and it stretches from Prestatyn (Walk no. 3) in the north to Llandegla (Walk no. 11) in the south, 35km/22 miles in all. The high ground is heather moorland with fast streams flowing through bracken-covered lower slopes and on through deciduous woodland of native oak, birch and ash. There are also Forestry Commission conifer plantations. This varied habitat of 62 square miles supports much wildlife, including badgers and hares, lizards and adders, kestrel, merlin, siskin and both red and black grouse.

(2) There are altogether six hill forts on the Clwydian range, the largest of which is Penycloddiau just to the north of Moel Arthur. As is evident, they were defensible settlements built on top of hills. The forts still show clearly the concentric rings of ditches and walls which made them formidable obstacles but extra defences, in the form of wooden palisades on the easier slopes, have disappeared. Archaeologists have traced on many of them evidence of these, and of the circular wooden huts in which the inhabitants of each clan of the Deceangli lived. Many, including Moel Arthur, have yielded Romano-Brythonic pottery (3), evidence of long occupation since they are believed to have been constructed first about 2500 years ago. At one time they would have been a refuge from the Romans after many years of growth. The first settlers built their simple huts on a hilltop, and following generations extended the defences by building earthbanks from the ditches that they excavated. Moel Arthur, like all the forts, has only one entrance with guard chambers inside. There is no evidence for any connection with King Arthur who, while more than simply a legend, has left very few hard facts behind him. He was evidently an early soldier-king of the 6th century who united the Celts against the Saxons after the departure of the Romans from Britain but in subsequent years attracted around him the hopes of his countrymen for freedom. A vast body of literature has developed, from Malory's 'Morte d'Arthur' of 1485 to Disney's screen version of 'The Sword in the Stone'.

(3) Three artefacts of particular importance have been found on other

sites in NE Wales. The first was a bronze age collar or 'torc' found in 1816 at Caerwys just to the north and used as a gate fastening until a gypsy recognised its value. It was made of Irish gold in about 1200 BC and was circular with a circumference of over 1.3m/50" and a weight of 0.7kg/26 oz. The Marquis of Westminster bought it for his home near Chester. The second was a gold ceremonial bowl, made in black oak in the shape of a boat and covered in gold decoration. It is over 3000 years old and may be seen in the National Museum of Wales in Cardiff. The third was found near Mold in 1833 on a hill called Bryn yr Ellyllon or Mound of the Fairies. Around the skeleton of a chieftain was a ceremonial cape of leather, entirely covered with embossed gold, again almost 3000 years old. A facsimile is in Cardiff, but the original is in the British Museum. If our impression of these ancient peoples was one of primitive tribes then these discoveries must surely make us reassess our views. The society which produced them must have been highly organised and very sophisticated. A feature of the discovery of the cape which I find intriguing is that the excavations were made because there had long been stories about a ghostly rider dressed in golden armour haunting this hill. This would seem to be clear evidence of folk memory passing on a story for over 3000 years with some truth still persisting at the end of that time.

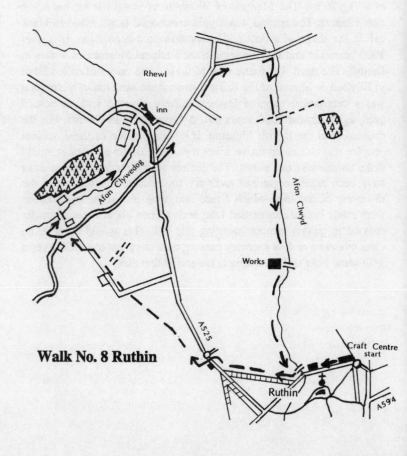

Walk No. 8 Ruthin

Rhewl

inn

Afon Clywedog

Afon Clwyd

Works

A525

Craft Centre start

Ruthin

A594

Ruthin – the last uprising

OS Map No.:	116
Start:	G.R. 125585. Car parks near the signposted Craft Centre.
Access:	Ruthin is at the junction of the A525 and the A494. It is on the No. 51 bus route, Rhyl/Corwen and the D8 from Wrexham.
Facilities:	Toilets and café in Craft Centre, restaurants and pubs in town.

Amount of climbing: 50m/165ft.

Ruthin town centre has many interesting buildings (1) and was the scene of the opening battle in the uprising of Owain Glyndŵr (2). The walk gives outstanding views of the Clwydian Hills, featured in other walks in this book, as well as taking you along the banks of two lovely rivers.

Walk Directions: (-) denotes Point of Interest

Leave the craft centre and turn right. After 300m/330 yards you pass the blue-painted premises of Richard Williams, Builders' Merchant and cross the Afon Clwyd. On the right is an iron kissing gate. Go through this and cross a little footbridge. Keep on the left of the field and go past a children's playground, through a sports ground and then a field, keeping to the left all the time.

After about 800m/½ mile you will reach the A525. Turn right and walk until you are opposite a filling station. Cross the road and go through the metal farm gate that you will see. Keep to the left of the field and go through the next gate you reach. Turn right and go uphill with the hedge on your right until you come to a gate. Go through this and continue uphill but with the hedge now on your left. Further stiles will bring you to a farm access road which you cross to a stile on the far side. Keep going in the same direction, the hedges still on your left. (The OS map shows the right of way as going up the farm drive, but this is not correct). You pass the farm itself over to your left and then a little pond on the right. Do not follow the more obvious track to the right.

Where the hedge makes a little 'dog-leg to the right is a rather dilapidated stile which you cross before continuing down to a stile on a lane, the hedge to your right now. Cross the lane half left to a stony track which passes a house and then zig-zags down to a footbridge over the Afon Clywedog. Turn right on a stony track through woodland and beautiful limestone outcrops. It is, in fact, worth turning left for a while to savour this gorge a little more before turning back. If you do this, look out for two well preserved lime kilns (3) on the right. You will recognise two stone structures with large openings with iron bars across.

Several local people told me that this track was called Lady Bagot's Drive (4). It brings you past some houses and a farm to a lovely packhorse bridge and then to the A525 again. Cross to the Drovers' Arms and turn right. At the end of the village, about 200m/220 yards, turn left on a lane and stay on this for about a mile, passing a turning to the right and then two to the left.

You will reach a bridge over the Afon Clwyd, but do not cross it. Turn right and follow the river bank which will be on your left. There are numerous stiles, most of them next to the river but some a few metres to the right and at one point the path makes its way round the sewage works. Just keep as near to the river as you can and after 2.4km/1.5 miles you will reach the little bridge that you crossed at the start of the walk. Go over it to the kissing gate and the road; turn left and you will soon be back at the Craft Centre.

Points of Interest:

(1) With the help of a town plan obtainable from the tourist office you can easily locate these buildings. The mediaeval castle, predictably one of Edward I's, is to be seen only in the towers and part of the curtain wall. The remainder is a new house built in 1826 and enlarged in 1849. In 1921 the family sold the house which became a clinic. It is

now a hotel which also offers mediaeval banquets. The gardens are very agreeable to wander round and can be enjoyed after taking afternoon tea in the tea-rooms which are open to non-residents.

To the front of St Peter's Church in the main square are gates designed by the Davies brothers of Croesfoel near Wrexham. Their work also includes gates at St Giles Church in Wrexham, Chirk Castle and Erddig Hall (Walk no. 13). The church has two naves, the north given by Henry VII in gratitude to the Welsh who helped him take the throne at the Battle of Bosworth in 1485. Its 480 carved oak panels are lit by a switch that you can find near the hymn board. Behind the church, which has cloisters remaining from its origins as a monastery, are the almshouses (Christ's Hospital) and the old grammar school.

Also worth looking for are the clock tower in the square; the Town Hall in Castle Street with its sculptures; the Myddleton Arms with its seven dormer windows called the 'Eyes of Ruthin'; and the adjacent 18th century Castle Hotel. Barclays Bank has outside it a stone known as Maen Huail. In a quarrel over a woman it seems that King Arthur was wounded in the thigh by Huail and given a permanent limp. When Huail later taunted him about it, Arthur had him beheaded on this very stone. There are many lovely half-timbered buildings in the town, including the NatWest bank, also in the square where you can see, if you look up under the eaves, the remains of the gibbet last used in 1679 to hang a Franciscan monk.

(2) On 20th September 1400, on the eve of the annual fair day, Ruthin was attacked, looted and destroyed by one Welshman whose name even today is known across the border – Owain Glyndŵr – or Owen Glendower as he appears in Shakespeare. Glyndŵr was one of the many aristocratic Welshmen of his period who were drawn to the English court because of its power and the opportunities that it offered. He had evidently studied law in London and had fought under Richard II against the Scots at Berwick in 1385. With these ties he might seem an unlikely candidate to lead a revolution against the English throne, but there was unrest in Wales over the way in which the new King, Henry IV, had usurped the throne from Richard II, and discontent among an impoverished peasantry. Although the details are not clear,

it seems that a dispute over land with a neighbour, Lord Grey of Ruthin, in which Glyndŵr was proclaimed a traitor, sparked the revolt.

After his attack on Ruthin, Glyndŵr was proclaimed Prince of Wales at his home in Glyndyfrdwy, near Corwen. His descent from the princes of Powys and from Lord Rhys of Deheubarth gave him credibility in the eyes of his compatriots and he was without doubt a charismatic leader. In the following year he took Conwy castle and won a great battle near Machynlleth. In their turn the English burnt his two homes at Glyndyfrdwy and Sycharth but Glyndŵr retaliated with his capture of Harlech Castle which he made his headquarters. In 1403 he made a treaty with the French whom he told how his people had 'been trodden underfoot by the fury of the barbarous Saxons'.

By 1404 English rule in Wales had become confined to some castles and to small areas on the coast and Glyndŵr was able to show that he was no simple guerilla leader. He held his own parliament at Machynlleth and drew up plans for a Welsh legal system and church and for two universities, the basis of a completely independent Wales.

His plans were not to be realised, however, for English pressure increased, the French withdrew their support and castles were re-taken. By 1410 Glyndŵr was a fugitive but it says much for his standing and for his people that he was never betrayed, despite the offer of many rewards. What finally happened to him is not known; his last appearance is said to have been at the Pillar of Elyseg near Llangollen (Walk no. 14) and tradition has it that he spent his last years with his daughter in Herefordshire, refusing a pardon from Henry V. The best place to learn about Glyndŵr is in his Parliament House in Machynlleth and you might consider walking the Glyndŵr Way.

Although the rebellion failed, Glyndŵr is still a potent hero in Wales and still retains the aura remembered in Shakespeare's time nearly 200 years after his disappearance from the records as possessing magical powers. As a symbol of Welsh nationhood he has few equals.

(3) Lime has been burnt since prehistoric times, a kiln dating from 2500 BC having been excavated in Mesopotamia. Its use has been widespread, from preparing leather and in medicine but it is most

commonly used in building and in agriculture. Everywhere you walk in limestone areas in Britain you can see kilns, some like these two, in good condition, most now collapsing. These kilns date from the late 18th and the 19th centuries, coming between the periods of simpler, often temporary structures and later industrialised units. The calcium in the lime encourages plant growth, but adding lime also counters the acidity in the soil. The fine lime powder needed was obtained by burning the raw limestone in the kilns and then slaking it with water when it would crumble. In addition to those built for commercial use many farms had their own kilns, and when a large structure, like a castle, was being built a kiln was usually built first to provide lime for the mortar. One of the first accounts in Britain of a kiln for agricultural lime is from Wales, George Owen's 'Description of Pembrokeshire', 1603.

(4) The Bagot family is a prominent one in this area, Bishop Bagot of St Asaph having had the front of the Bishop's palace built in 1791. They owned several houses in the district and this drive seems to lead to Pool Park, just off the B5105, built in 1828 for Lord Bagot of Blithfield. At the top of Clocaenog Forest to the south-west at G.R. 064552 is a monument of 1830 with an inscription to William, second Lord Bagot, who was responsible for the planting.

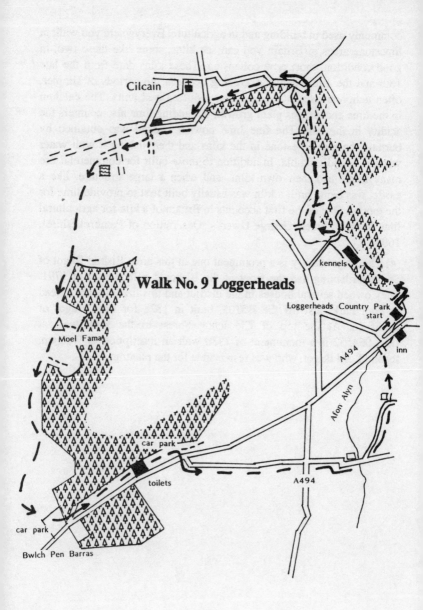

Cilcain

kennels

Walk No. 9 Loggerheads

Loggerheads Country Park
start

Moel Fama

inn

Afon Alyn

car park

A494

toilets

A494

car park

Bwlch Pen Barras

At Loggerheads

OS Map No.:   116

Start: G.R. 197626 Loggerheads Country Park (1 & 2).

Access: Loggerheads is on the A494 Mold/Ruthin road.
                     Bus no. 31, Mold/Cilcain and B5, Mold/Ruthin.

Facilities: Information Centre, toilets, café, pub.

Amount of climbing: 350m/1100ft.

This is a longer walk than most others in the book but it has no steep
gradients except for one short stretch. An alternative is suggested if
you want just an easy route to the summit of Moel Fama – and why
not? The market town of Mold (3) makes an interesting visit before or
after your exertions.

Walk Directions: (-) denotes Point of Interest

From the car park cross the little bridge leading to the Information
Centre. Go round it, past the café and toilets and then the craft centre,
outdoor shop and education centre. Cross the stone bridge across the
River Alun and turn left. You now follow the river on your left on a
wide, gravelled path, the Leete Path (4) to a wooden kissing gate. Go
through this onto a rougher track which will stay level for 1.5 miles as
the river drops below you. Past some boarding kennels the track is
again wide and stony as far as a white iron gate. Cross the lane onto
the signposted continuation of the track beneath trees. The leat is now
quite clear and you will pass a number of caves which are the remains
of mining activity. One cave is passed by a bridge and another
footpath crosses soon after. The path ends at a lane.

Turn left and go downhill to cross the river by a narrow road
bridge. Continue uphill and where the road turns right, take the
footpath signposted on the left. A series of waymarked stiles leads to a
junction with a bridleway near a bridge. Turn right, uphill, pass a pond

and you reach a lane where you turn left. There is, however, a convenient bench a few yards to the right, while Cilcain village with its pub and church is only a few minutes away in the same direction.

The walk continues downhill passing a cottage called 'Wayside' and climbing up to a T junction where you turn right along a narrow lane. A few yards past a grey, metal-clad building the metalled road turns right. Go through a gateway on the left and then cross a signposted stone stile on the right only a few yards along the track. Cross two fields, the second stile bringing you to a stony track. Cross it and go along the stony track almost directly opposite so that you keep in the same direction. After passing through a gate the bridleway, now grassy, passes a small reservoir and continues steadily uphill with fences variously on the left, right or both sides. Another track joins from the right and goes off left after you cross a stream. Follow the signposted route.

After a second stream, a steep climb takes you up a zigzag path with some fencing, to a junction with a bridleway at the corner of a coniferous wood. An old stone wall here provides a welcome seat from which to admire the scenery. Follow the line of the plantation uphill and remains of the Jubilee Tower on the summit (5) will soon come into sight.

The route down is roughly in the same direction. A broad stony track leads down for 2.4km/1.5 miles, following a stone wall at first. Whenever there is a fork in the path just follow the white acorn markers of Offa's Dyke path until you reach the car park at Bwlch Pen Barras (6) where there is usually an ice cream van. Cross a stile on the left side of the car park and go over a forestry track onto a grassy path following the power lines with the road to your right. This will bring you down to a toilet block. Go to the left of the toilets, cross a bridge and walk straight through the car park and picnic area ahead, and out the other end onto a rough track, still parallel to the road until you see another lane joining from the right. Cross and go along this lane.

After a mile you reach the A494. Cross with care and continue on the lane opposite until you come to a bridge. Just over this turn left up another lane and when this goes to the right at the top of a rise, go left up the gravelled drive with a bridleway signposted. This leads down to the A494 which you cross. Turn right for the country park.

For a shorter walk, drive south-west on the A494. After 1.6km/ 1 mile, where the main road takes a sharp bend to the left, go straight ahead on a minor road where a car park is signposted. There are toilets and picnic tables here (G.R. 172611). Follow the Blue waymarkers uphill to the summit. From there you can either retrace your steps or follow the directions from (6) above. An even shorter ascent can be made by parking at the Bwlch (G.R. 161606) and walking north along Offa's Dyke Path.

Points of Interest:

(1) The Country Park with its unusual name (2) was bought in 1974 by the County Council from the Crosville Motor Company which had developed the business of day trips to the country since the thirties. There had been not only a wooden café that many of us remember with affection, but also a bandstand and boating lake. This was as far as you could reasonably get in a day by public transport from Merseyside. There are now industrial and nature trails, crafts, a mill, an outdoor shop and many popular events in a crowded programme.

(2) The name Loggerheads is commemorated in the sign outside the Inn opposite the Country Park – 'We three Loggerheads'. If you are wondering where the third one is, it is allegedly the person looking at the sign! The sign, now obviously not original, is reputed to have been the work of Richard Wilson (3). It is named after a boundary dispute between the Grosvenor Estate and the Lords of Mold. This was evidently acrimonious, but not without purpose as much mineral wealth (4) was at stake. The monument built over the boundary stone in question is on the left hand side of the road in the Mold direction and not far from the park on the Flintshire/Denbighshire border. The stone is said to have the footprint of King Arthur's horse, made when it leapt from the summit of Moel Fama.

(3) Richard Wilson was an 18th century landscape artist much admired by both Constable and Turner and a co-founder of the Royal

Academy. A famous painting of his – Snowdon from Llyn Nantlle Uchaf – hangs in the Walker Art Gallery in Liverpool and another, equally well known, of Cadair Idris is in the Tate. Wilson was born in 1714 near Machynlleth and died at Colomendy Hall on the other side of the road from here in 1782. He died poor, dependent upon the charity of relatives, and was buried near the north wall of the churchyard of St Mary's in Mold, where there is a commemorative window. Here also is the grave of Daniel Owen (1836-95), a novelist in the Welsh language whose main theme was the lives of the working poor. Outside the library you can see his statue and inside, a museum devoted to his life and works. His attitude is expressed on the statue: 'Not for the wise and learned have I written but for the common people', an attitude that made him less than popular with the leaders of the Methodist church. The realism with which he wrote popularised the novel in Welsh, and his subject matter led to a tradition of such novels, including the well-known *How Green was my Valley* by Richard Llywelyn.

(4) A leat is an artificial watercourse. The eccentric spelling 'leete' is, as far as I know, an entirely local usage. All along the Leete Path are the signs of industrial activity, if you know what to look for. Fortunately, there is a trail with a guide to help out, for it is almost impossible for us to realise the nature and extent of the workings on such sites. Here, for instance, the shafts went down 180m/600' and at nearby Halkyn, one of the last lead mines in Britain to be in production, they were twice that depth. Water wheels provided power for pumps to keep the mines dry, for flooding was one of the major problems encountered. At 12m/40' in diameter these were not as large as the Laxey wheel in the Isle of Man but must have been impressive nonetheless. An additional problem here was that the river flowed into underground channels in the limestone just where it was needed. This still happens every summer. The answer was to build a leat to supply water to the wheels and it is this that the first part of the walk follows. The path stays level while the river on your left falls away rapidly.

Nature has been kind to the spoil heaps and mine entrances and further on in the walk you will see just how big some of these were.

The work was hard and monotonous, the miners having to climb down wooden ladders to reach their workplace. Rheumatism and chest complaints were common, the result of the cold, wet and muddy conditions underground. Conditions above ground, while in some respects easier, were still hard. Dressing the ore, pushing wagons, operating the windlasses and so on, were often jobs for women and children in the days before mechanisation, and there would have been little shelter for the twelve or thirteen hour shift.

(5) The stonework on the summit (554m/1818') is what is left of a 35m/115 foot high tower built in 1810, in a vaguely Egyptian style, to commemorate the Golden Jubilee of the reign of George III. Drawings still exist of the tower which was never quite completed, and which lost its top section in a storm in 1862. It lay in ruins until 1969 when, for the investiture of the present Prince of Wales, the contractors for the St Asaph by-pass, the A55, made it safe. In European Conservation Year, 1970, a viewing platform was added, together with four plaques describing the surrounding landscape.

(6) The pass was the dividing point of two glaciers flowing NE/SW. It was formerly a drovers' road and in the 18th century, a turnpike. An inn and stables formerly stood on the site of the car park.

Walk No. 10 Hawarden

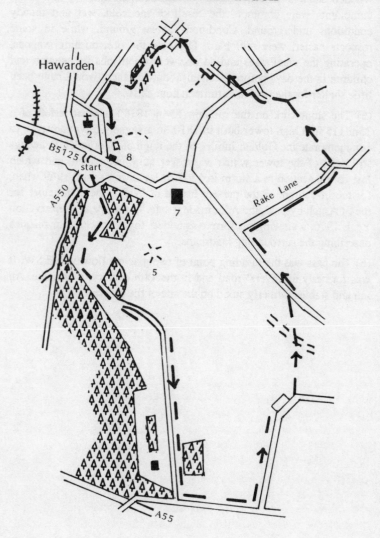

Hawarden – home of Gladstone

OS Map No.:	117
Start:	G.R. 316657, public car park south of the road junction.
Access:	Hawarden is at the A550/B5125 junction, and on the Birkenhead/Wrexham line.
Facilities:	There are pubs, shops and public toilets on the main street.

Amount of climbing: 60m/200ft.

Hawarden, although it is on the edge of an industrialised area of NE Wales [including nearby Buckley (1)], is a town with many attractive features. The church (2), and St Deiniol's library (3) are both notable, having associations with W. E. Gladstone (4).

Walk Directions: (-) denotes Point of Interest

At the back of the car park, opposite the main entrance, is a footpath sign which will lead you down a narrow path. As soon as the ground levels out, look for the remains of an 18th century corn mill on the left – the mill wheel looks relatively intact. As you cross the stream there are remains of a sluice gate on the right. Cross the stile by the gate in front of you. The path now wanders through beautiful beech woodland, and crosses several other tracks but it is always well signposted with a yellow arrow and a Ranger Service Circular Walk sign. You will be following the estate wall to begin with.

When the woodland gives way to open fields, on your left, look out for the remains of Hawarden's old castle (5). In the same direction you can see the Stanlow oil refineries and, behind them, Helsby Hill. After 800m/½ mile you come to a gate leading to a track between hedges. As you leave the woods notice directly ahead of you, in the distance, the isolated hill on which stands Beeston Castle (6). A further 800m/½ mile brings you to the entrance to Cherry Orchard house which is on our right. In the field on your left at this point is an uncommon tree, the Lucombe oak, which is evergreen.

After 400m/¼ mile you reach a quiet lane, now by-passed by the A55. Cross to the footpath and turn left. In 800m/½ mile turn left on a signposted track which leads over several gates and stiles to a farm which you pass to its surfaced access road. This last section is very muddy.

The farm lane soon turns sharply right and in a corner to the left are two footpath signs by a gate and stile. Cross the stile and walk parallel to the telephone wires ahead of you. To your left you can see the 'new' Hawarden Castle (7) among the trees. As you begin to drop towards a stream, turn left under the wires towards the corner of the field where behind a large oak tree is a footbridge.

From here, posts with faded yellow paint guide you uphill and towards the left, through a plantation of young evergreens to a stile; a plantation of deciduous trees; and another plantation of more mature evergreens. To the right of one stile is what looks like a WWII bunker. Cross some moss-covered concrete foundations to an arable field across which, half left, you will see a signpost and stile. This is reached by whatever gaps in the crops you can find. You may be lucky enough to come at strawberry time.

You are now on the B5125 which can be busy during the week, as to your right is Hawarden airport and aircraft factory on the industrial estate. Cross to the footpath and turn left. In 1.2km/¾ mile you come to Rake Lane where you turn right. The farm shop on the other side of the road here sells ice cream, but is not open all year round. After 800m/½ mile you pass on your left Croft Cottage. Here, where the road turns sharp right, go over the stile by the gate on the left and follow the hedge on your right, the new castle again visible across the fields on the left.

Maintain direction over stiles and a footbridge of railway sleepers until you have to cross a stile on the right. In a few m/yards, cross a stile on the left and then a third. Keep the hedge on your left and cross two stiles by gates until you reach a lane. Turn left here and take the first turning on the right. Immediately past the farm buildings, look for a stile on the left and then turn right following the hedge on your right. Cross further stiles, maintaining this direction until you reach an estate of new houses, passing between two of them to the road. Cross and go to the next stile between houses numbers eight and ten. You are now on an embankment among trees. Continue, go over another stile and keep the hedge to your right until you reach a kissing gate on the road.

Turn left, pass between the cemeteries and turn left at the T junction. Pass the schools and at the top of the hill have a quick look at the lock-up (8) on the corner of the High Street. Turn right to reach the monument. The car park is just down to the left.

Points of Interest:

(1) The nearby town of Buckley was noted for its bricks and its pottery, the raw materials – clay, lead and coal – being abundant on Buckley Mountain. There is evidence that pottery had been produced in this area since mediaeval times, but it was in the late 17th and early 18th centuries that the trade came into prominence. Kilns were built and operated by family units, and so the production was essentially small scale. Nonetheless, Buckley pottery was traded throughout Wales and exported to Ireland, good use being made of easy access to harbours. Wheels and moulds were used to produce domestic wares such as bowls, jars and tankards, and at one time designs were scratched into the surfaces. The best known products were large plates with simple patterns on. Later came coarser, black-glazed kitchen ware. The North Walian Art Pottery, which closed in 1929, introduced some Art Nouveau designs. The library in Buckley has a collection of local pottery (telephone 01244 549210 for opening times).

(2) The church, which was rebuilt by Sir Gilbert Scott after a fire in 1857, contains a huge monument to W.E. Gladstone, the English Liberal statesman. It takes the form of a marble ship containing sculptures of Gladstone and his wife, both of whom are actually buried in Westminster Abbey. Another memorial are the windows by Burne-Jones, the last he was to design, depicting a nativity scene.

(3) St Deiniol's Library, an attractive sandstone building, is well signposted, but unfortunately cannot be visited. It is another memorial

to Gladstone, his own idea, and contains 32,000 books which he donated before his death. It is residential, its main purpose being theological study.

(4) W.E. Gladstone was four times Prime Minister, a record equalled only in recent times. His legislation included an education act and an electoral reform act. He also advocated home rule for Ireland but failed to achieve it. He was also a classical scholar and a writer on affairs of the church.

(5) The site of the old castle dominates the marshlands around Chester, and has been fortified since pre-Roman times. The present castle was built in the 13th century and was used by Edward I as a base for his invasion of Wales. On Palm Sunday 1282, the second War of Independence was started when the castle was taken by Dafydd, brother of Llywelyn ap Gruffudd, Prince of Wales. It was defended by the Parliamentary side in the Civil War and suffered severe damage. Restoration took place in the 19th century. You may visit the ruins by entering the park by the gate near the car park.

(6) Beeston Castle is 15 miles away in Cheshire. It was built in 1220 by Randle Blundeville, Earl of Chester. On his death it became crown property, and was extended by both Henry III and Edward II. The hill on which it stands is 100m/330' high, and it was a formidable structure. By the time of the Civil War, though, it was already in ruins. The nearby Peckforton Hills contain a 19th century mock castle used in the 1990's for a film of Robin Hood.

(7) The new castle became the home of Gladstone after his marriage to Catherine Glynne, heiress to the Hawarden estate, and is still the home of the Gladstone family. It was originally a building in the classical style, dating from 1752 and designed by Joseph Turner, a local architect whose house, The Elms, is on the main street. At the turn of the 19th century the house was remodelled as a castle. When Gladstone took over the house, he had an extra tower built which contained his private study. The castle is occasionally open to view, but the parkland may be visited at any time from the Leopold Gate, the

red-painted gate near the car park. The gates close at 7pm in winter, 9pm in summer.

(8) The stone lock-up was also designed by Joseph Turner.

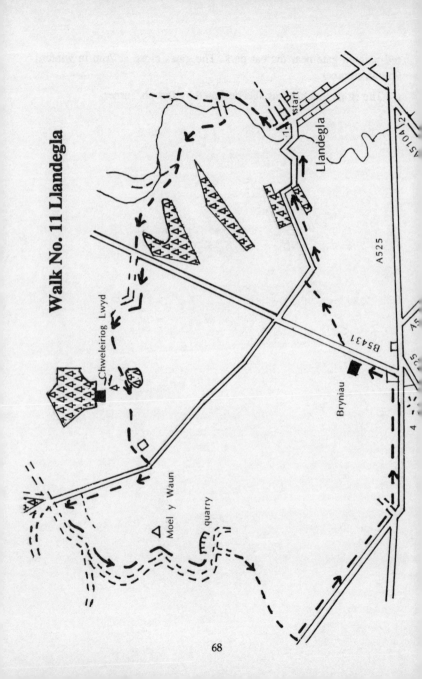

Walk No. 11 Llandegla

start

Llandegla

A525

B5431

Bryniau

Chweleiriog Lwyd

Moel y Waun

quarry

A5104/2

Llandegla – the drove-roads

OS Map No.:	116
Start:	G.R. 196523 a small car park near the church (1).
Access:	Llandegla is on the A525 Wrexham/Ruthin road. Buses 91, Carrog/Wrexham and D8, Wrexham/Ruthin.
Facilities:	The Crown Inn (2) is on the A525 within 0.5ml. The village post office has a small café.

Amount of climbing: 100m/330ft.

This walk is at the very southern end of the Clwydian range in very peaceful limestone countryside. It is difficult now to envisage the busy place this must once have been, for Llandegla was once the point where several drove-roads (3) joined, before climbing the hill to Llangollen *en route* for en route for England.

Walk Directions: (-) denotes Point of Interest

Turn right from the car park and take the little cul-de-sac to the right of the church. This leads down to a gate and Offa's Dyke signposts, which lead roughly round the left-hand side of a meadow before reaching a bridge which you cross. Turn half right and follow the right-hand edge of the field; the exit is over a waymarked stile well concealed on the right. Continue with the fence now on your left; cross a ladder stile, the fence now on your right for a few m/yards, and then on your left. Cross another footbridge to a stile by a gate, turn left and after a few m/yards go right, continuing to the corner of the field. Turn left at the signpost, and along a track between hedges which leads to a lane.

Cross onto the access road to Chweleiriog Lwyd and stay on it until, just over a cattle grid, the waymarkers direct you to the left and up to two stiles and a third tucked away in the corner of the field.

Cross and turn left as directed, following the hedge up to a lane where you turn right.

The lane descends to the junction of six paths with a wood just ahead. Cross the stile immediately on the left by a gate, and walk on a green path contouring the hillside with a fence on your left, and lovely views along the Vale of Clwyd. Just past a gate the track divides, the left fork rising and passing through a gate. There is no waymark and no stile, so just climb this gate and follow the green track which has a fence on the right. It winds around the hillside for 800m/½ mile and goes through a gate not long after which it drops to a small quarry. Turn to the right, downhill and through a gateway onto a rough track. Beyond the second gate the track peters out but keep in the same direction on a cattle trod and you will soon see the next gate, and beyond it a short enclosed section of track. When this turns sharply right, follow the reassuring sign 'footpath' through two gates ahead. A short steep descent leads to a lane. Cross with care and turn left, staying on the lane for about 1.6km/1 mile, passing the road to Pentre Celyn at the top of the rise. Watch out on the right for the remains of Castell y Rhodwydd (4) a little before the junction with the B5431.

At this junction, turn left towards Llanarmon-yn-Iâl and a short way past the entrance to Bryniau, go through the metal gate on the right and then diagonally left across the field to a second gate by an ash tree. Go straight across the next field to a gate where you turn right and follow the lane all the way back to Llandegla. The map shows various routes across the fields but at present they are not traceable on the ground.

Points of Interest:

(1) The most interesting feature of the church is the east window which was made in 1800, originally for St Asaph Cathedral, by a well known glass painter of his time, Francis Eginton of Birmingham. The little angels, or putti, who hold the emblems of the Passion are most unlike those usually found in churches, and seem to be based on the pagan cupids on the wall-paintings in Pompeii.

(2) The Crown Inn has the distinction of once having served afternoon

tea to the Prime Minister W.E. Gladstone and his wife, who were touring the district in their carriage. The Prime Minister was highly regarded in Wales, despite his social class, nationality and High-Church affiliations (see Walk no. 10).

(3) The driving of cattle and other animals from Wales into England began to become highly organised after about 1570, in the Tudor period, and was killed off by about 1870 when the railway system was fully developed. However, since it must have taken a long time to evolve, and since it is known that there were still some Welsh drovers in the 1930's, we can safely say that the trade lasted for well over 500 years. Unlike mining and quarrying, or even the now defunct railways themselves, there is very little trace of the activity of the drovers to be seen, but it was arguably at least as important an economic and social factor as any.

In the Tudor period, London's population had grown to 50,000, and there was a great demand for meat in England's first substantial urban development. This demand was met by the rearing of beef cattle, not only in Wales of course, but also in Scotland and northern England. From each of these areas the cattle were driven to London by routes which had to be worked out. The animals had to be shod, fed and rested, and the drovers themselves needed accommodation and ways of finding the routes, for which there were no maps. More significantly, ways had to be developed of moving credit as well as money.

From this it can readily be seen that there sprang up a system of waymarking the routes, along which there were inns, pastures and shoeing stations. Not so immediately obvious is the fact that the needs of the drovers and their clients was a strand in the development of the banking system, which ranks with that of later industrial activity and overseas trade.

Our first search for the signs of droving must be with the inns, for there are in Wales many Drovers' Arms like the one on the A525 just north of Ruthin (see Walk no. 8). Others may have changed their names, but many must have been simply an extension of a farm where the beer sold was surplus to domestic needs. Llandegla itself once had eleven inns, while Llanarmon-yn-Iâl, 4km/2½ miles to the north, had ten. Our second search is by courtesy of the archaeologist – for example, when petrol pumps were being installed by the Raven Inn in Llanarmon about thirty years ago, many of the cues (shoes) worn by the cattle were found. Similarly we need professional help to know where the roads were, since so many of them have now been incorporated into the present road network. Having said that, you can be fairly certain that you are on a drove-road if it is wider than necessary, with the hedges or walls leaving very wide verges. The cattle were not hurried along but needed time and room to graze. The third sign to look for would be a group of three Scots pines planted by the farmers providing accommodation as a sign to the drovers, but I am afraid that I have looked in vain – they may have been there but have probably gone by now.

The trade was considerable, the herds being described by John Williams, Archbishop of York, as 'the Spanish fleet of Wales, which brings hither the little gold and silver that we have'. Some cattle were driven to Northampton, where the hides were used in the leather industry. In 1620 £12,000 worth of butter was sent from Glamorgan to Bristol. London, though, was the main market, and geese and pigs were also common on the routes. As towns expanded, the trade grew and became central to the Welsh economy – in the 18th century a partnership of drovers from Llyn had a turnover of £16,000. A rural population moved from a subsistence economy, where crops and cattle were for their own consumption and money was little used, to one where trade and the exchange of goods for cash was the norm.

In this the drovers played the central role, the majority honestly, some evidently not. The drover not only moved the cattle, he had to get the best price for it and bring the money back. In time, systems of credit developed because of the presence of murderous bandits on the return journey, and there were very early Welsh banks, many of which were absorbed by Martins Bank, itself taken over in the 1970's by Barclays. Another way of reducing the amount of cash carried was for the drovers to carry out business on behalf of their customers. Many wealthy Welsh families had sons at Oxford or at the Inns of Court in

London, training for the legal professions. The costs of their tuition, lodgings and other upkeep could be taken from the money raised by selling cattle at Smithfield market. There were taxes such as the ship tax which could be settled in a similar way, so that the head drovers became negotiators and businessmen. They were also better informed about the outside world than those who stayed at home, and carried the latest news back with them – the victory at Waterloo, for instance. It should be no surprise that their earnings were 15 times that of a labourer.

There are many interesting little aspects of their life that you can read about. The dogs used for driving cattle were corgis which are quick, intelligent and aggressive, their size and speed enabling them to nip at the heels of the cattle and move out of the way just as smartly. Stories are told of how the drovers sent their dogs home once they had reached their destination, often as far away as Kent, sold their ponies and started the long trek back once their business was complete. The dogs would find their own way back before the men, and preparations would begin for the expected return of the master of the house!

(4) All that can be seen are the remains of an embankment of what was a motte and bailey – the motte being a mound with a ditch round it and a wooden defensive structure on top, and the bailey a further enclosed area with a wooden fence all round. This one was built by Owain Gwynedd in the mid 12th century.

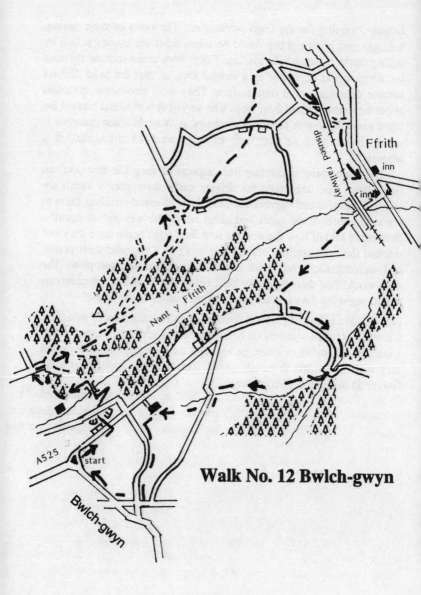

Walk No. 12 Bwlch-gwyn

Ffrith

inn

inn

disused railway

Nant Y Ffrith

A525

start

Bwlch-gwyn

Bwlch-gwyn – the highest village in Wales

OS Map No.:　　　　117

Start:　　　　　　　　G.R. 263536, the War Memorial in Bwlch-gwyn.

Access:　　　　　　　Bwlch-gwyn is on the A525 to Ruthin off the
　　　　　　　　　　　A438, Wrexham by-pass. Buses: D8, E12 and 91
　　　　　　　　　　　Wrexham-Corwen.

Facilities:　　　　　　Shop and several pubs in Bwlch-gwyn; two pubs
　　　　　　　　　　　in Ffrith.

Amount of climbing: 270m/900ft.

The countryside around the Nant y Ffrith valley is very attractive, its
quarries now grown over, its lead mines long exhausted. It is just on
the fringe of the early lead and iron mines of the Clywedog Valley (1)
and the great coalmining areas surrounding Wrexham. The village of
Ffrith shows evidence of Roman occupation (2) and the area is crossed
by-drove roads and packhorse trails (3).

Walk Directions:　　　　　　　　　　(-) denotes Point of Interest

From the war memorial go down the little lane running downhill off
the A525 in a north-westerly direction. Just past some stone cottages
turn left at a footpath sign, on a path leading between quarries to a
lane. Cross, and take the signposted path down over two forest tracks,
following red marks on the trees. At the third track turn left to reach a
bridge. Cross and turn left. Go over the stile on the right before the
large house (4) and continue uphill, over a metal gate and then
between fern covered stone walls to a lane where you turn right and go
through a gate onto a gravelled track.

After about 90m/100 yards the track forks, and in the centre is a
smaller green path going straight ahead. Take this path which has
mossy walls on both sides. There is one fork right which you ignore.

When you reach a large forestry track, cross and continue uphill on the track ahead. The old stone wall appears on your left intermittently, but it has vanished on the right with the felling of the trees. At the top of the rise when the track goes sharply left, keep straight ahead on a smaller path through a patch of silver birch and an outcrop of boulders.

A stile leads to a broad, grassy track between turfed stone walls, and to a second stile beyond which the walls are a good 18m/20 yards apart, typical of a drove-road (5). Green arrows in this section indicating the route have been sprayed over, making them difficult to see. Gradually a stony track develops leading down to a lane where you turn right.

In 45m/50 yards cross a signposted stile on the left. Follow a double fence with a newly planted holly hedge. Pass through two gateways, the hedge now on your right. Further gates lead down to a lane by a farm. Half left across the lane, a signposted stile leads to a footpath. Cross a stile on the right after 45m/50 yards and go half left, which is due north, to a stile in a wire fence, and to another in the field corner. Cross the stile and then follow the hedge on your right to the lane.

Turn right (uphill) for 180m/200 yards and when the lane turns sharply, keep straight ahead (bridleway sign). Past two houses, the surfaced lane becomes stony and descends to a stream passing beneath the bridge of a disused railway (6). Before you reach the stream, cross a stile of tubular steel on the right. Follow the stream and go through a builder's yard to the Bluebell Inn. The village and the Poacher's Cottage Inn are to the left, but the route doubles back around the Bluebell to pass under the great railway arch. The path splits into three – take the left fork with the bridleway sign, cross a bridge and turn right. This is a gradually ascending, gravelled path – an old packhorse trail – which passes under the track of a quarry line, and reaches a lane after 800m/½ mile. Turn left and follow the lane until in 800m/½ mile it doubles back upon itself.

On the right is a footpath sign apparently pointing to nothing in particular. Cross the stream, and you will find a path which improves and goes up to some steps to a stile at the top of the wood. Cross this and another on the left, and then keep to the left of the fields until you come to a lane.

Turn left and in about 18m/20 yards go over a narrow stile on the right, and then diagonally left to a stile in the field corner. Keep to the field edge for 27m/30 yards before going through a signposted metal gate on the right. Walk up to the farm ahead, passing through two metal gates. Turn left and go through another gate and along the field to a kissing gate beneath power lines.

On the stony track turn left, and when you reach a crossroads by two little graveyards, turn right to the main road opposite the King's Head. Turn right again to reach the war memorial.

Points of Interest:

(1) As you come up the hill from Wrexham you will notice a number of brown tourist signposts on the left indicating archaeological sites. The Clywedog Valley was an important industrial area in the 18th century, and you will spot roads like Smelt Lane. The river was the power source for the hammers and bellows used in processing the local deposits of iron ore and lead but as elsewhere, coal became the energy source and the Clywedog Valley was left to return to nature. Now this patch of our history is being dug up, evaluated and put on show. An 11km/7 mile trail links the various sites, and you can get a leaflet from any of them.

One of the most interesting is Bersham ironworks whose products played a significant part in the American Civil War and the Napoleonic Wars. In 1775 an ironmaster from Cumbria, known as John 'Iron-mad' Wilkinson patented a method of boring out cylinders. Where cannon had been cast and then smoothed out they were now much more accurate. These weapons, together with shells, were supplied to both sides in the Russian-Turkist war of 1768, and to the Americans in the War of Independence – if we believe the rumours.

The method used was also suitable for casting and boring out cylinders for the new steam engines being developed by Watt and Boulton. In a dispute his sons, who had taken over from John, brought in gangs to smash up the works, and the family was ruined until a more modern works was set up nearby. The steam engines which they helped to develop were, in any case, to make water-powered factories such as Bersham redundant.

At nearby Croesfoel was the smithy where the Davies brothers produced the fantastically ornate gates which still grace many buildings in this area, such as Erddig Hall (see walk no. 13), Chirk Castle and Ruthin church (see walk no. 8).

(2) Ffrith village and its surrounding area have revealed much evidence of Roman occupation. Coins, rings, pins, amber beads, urns and an altar were found in 1828 when Offa's Dyke was levelled during roadworks. In the village itself, remains of a villa and two kilns have been uncovered, whilst various artefacts have turned up in local gardens.

(3) Packhorses have been used since Roman times, but became the common means of transportation in the 18th century. Northern England and Wales are criss-crossed by old trails, some of them now bridleways, others surfaced as part of the road network. The road to Cymau in Ffrith has a packhorse bridge over it, a few minutes walk from the Bluebell. A typical packhorse bridge has low parapets, to allow the passage of the horses with their large panniers slung low on each side. They frequently have recesses so that pedestrians can keep out of the way of the animals, whose coming was heralded by the jingling of the bells which they carried.

(4) This house was converted from the stables and coach house of Nant-y-Ffrith Hall, the foundations of which can be found if you turn right just after the bridge. In 1850 a hunting lodge was built here by a Liverpool tea merchant, Thomas Fry. Its next owner, also in the tea trade, sold it to a Mr Kyrke who built the hall. By 1950 a quarry company owned the estate, and the hall was pulled down.

(5) For more about drove-roads see walk no. 11.

(6) The railway was a branch of the Mold Railway, leading to limeworks at Ffrith. It opened in 1849 and was operated by the LNWR.

Erddig Hall – the time capsule

OS Map No.:	117
Start:	G.R. 328417, the car park at Erddig Hall.
Access:	Erddig is well signposted especially from the Wrexham by-pass but there is no public transport. You can, however, catch the no. 31 bus from Wrexham to Kings Mill, and start the walk there.
Facilities:	In Erddig Hall there are toilets and a café, but accessible only to National Trust members, or after paying the entrance fee.

Amount of climbing: 40m/130ft.

This is a lovely walk with lots of variety at all times of the year. There are woodlands and water meadows, and most of the time it is easy going underfoot. There is one short pull up from the river, but it is otherwise fairly level. If you enjoy visiting old houses then you will find Erddig a treat.

Walk Directions: (-) denotes Point of Interest

From the car park walk back along the driveway, passing the house entrance. Continue on the middle, tarmac path with an iron fence on your right, and fork right on a stony track which leads downhill. This route is signposted 'Cup and Saucer Waterfall'. Go through a gate, and cross a small wooden bridge on the left to see the Cup and Saucer and the hydraulic ram pump (1).

Go back over the bridge, turn left and continue on the track, crossing a stone bridge. Immediately before a second stone bridge, turn left and follow a gravel path signposted through several gateways. The river is to your right.

Pass between a house on your left and outbuildings on your right.

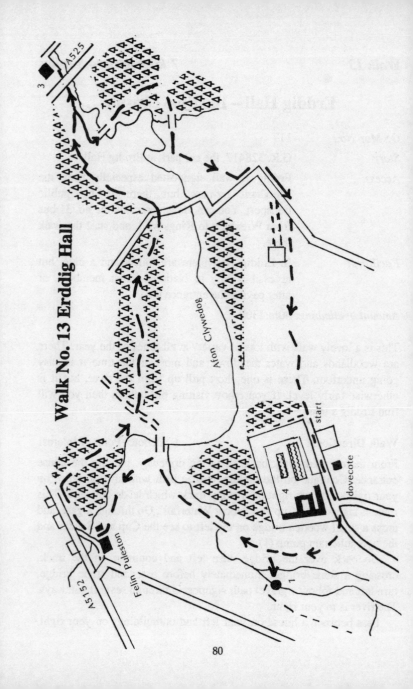

Walk No. 13 Erddig Hall

A525

3

Afon Clywedog

start

dovecote

4

Felin Puleston

A5152

(This is Felin Puleston, a former mill with a car park making an alternative start to the walk.) Turn right, cross a footbridge, go through a gate and take the left fork on a gravelled path with Clywedog Trail signs (2).

Stay on this gravel path. By a kissing gate another path joins from the right. Leave the wood by another kissing gate and turn left, keeping the fence on your left. Cross a gravelled track and go through a kissing gate, still following the Clywedog trail, on a path which is just inside the wood.

This leads to a kissing gate on a lane. Cross the lane to another gate on the far side, and continue through the wood. (Alternative car park and start on the right.) Eventually the path leads out of the wood by a stile. Turn left and keep the wood and stream on your left. Note over to the right a wooden footbridge which you can use to shorten the walk, as it is on the return route.

Follow the signposted route to the right to pass under the main road and visit Kings Mill (3). Return to this point and follow the riverside path to the bridge. Cross it and go uphill half right as signposted by a wire fence, before levelling out through a wood above the river.

Go down some wooden steps, cross a bridge and go up to a stile. Turn half right to the edge of the wood. Keep straight ahead as signposted. Pass a large oak tree to a post at the top of the rise, then keep to the right edge of the field as this will lead you directly to a stile onto a lane and avoid the very muddy area around the more obvious gate.

Turn left on the lane. The stile on the right is a short cut by a woodland path into the grounds of Erddig Hall (4). Keep on the lane, and 100m/110 yards past a farm entrance turn right and go through a kissing gate by a metal gate. Go through the gate ahead where there is rather a muddy patch, and walk in the same direction on the right hand side of the fields, through kissing gates, until you pass a tall hedge.

When you come to two kissing gates, still keep straight on and don't take the gate on the right. You should now see the dovecote by the car park, and the end of the walk.

Points of Interest:

(1) A ram pump is used to pump water to a higher level. It is a simple but ingenious device with few working parts, and requiring little maintenance. A board by the pump gives a detailed description of its workings and French origins, including the fact that its name is taken from the sound it makes, like two rams' heads meeting when they do battle. The Cup and Saucer is a semi-circular weir built to provide the pump with a head of water.

(2) King's Mill, at the eastern end of the Clywedog Trail, is now a Visitor Centre which has one of its two original waterwheels still working. You can watch corn being milled, and see an exhibition and video about the Clywedog valley.

(3) The Clywedog Trail is about 11km/7 miles long, and lies between Minera to the west and Kings Mill. It joins a number of archaeological sites concerned mainly with the iron industry, and is discussed in more detail in walk no. 12 Bwlch-gwyn.

(4) Erddig Hall and Cefn, to the north-east, are the only survivors of nine country houses which surrounded Wrexham, and of the many town houses belonging to the gentry. Wrexham has been especially prosperous since Tudor times, lying as it does between coalbearing areas and good agricultural land, both bringing wealth to the landowners. In the 18th century the balls held during the Wrexham season tempted many to leave London, and there were private theatres and fox-hunting as well. Erddig is our last witness to this wealth, for Wrexham has not fared well in the 19th and 20th centuries, becoming the victim of its own success. Period buildings, including many fine churches, can be sought out, but they now have no context. That Erddig survived to be handed over to the National Trust in 1973 is something of a miracle, and a story that can be appreciated fully only by a visit to the house.

The original house dates from 1687, but its construction ruined its owner who promptly sold it to one John Meller. He added the two wings and laid out the formal gardens. His nephew, Simon Yorke, inherited the house in 1733, and bought most of the furniture which you can see today. The Yorke family, the eldest sons always named Simon or Philip, remained here for nearly 250 years, and were noted for their interest in antiquities and in their servants. The house is full of portraits of the household staff and of poems written about them. They really do seem to have been appreciated. As nothing was ever discarded, the house is full of the lesser domestic objects that are often missing from other grand estates and the servants' quarters will be a memorable part of your visit. The house was never modernised in any way, no electricity, gas, running water or telephone, but it also suffered from neglect. Matters were brought to a head when the National Coal Board went back on an earlier agreement and mined the pillar of coal lying beneath the house, causing subsidence. The last owner, the delightfully eccentric Philip Yorke III, had no resources to restore it, and was even driven to sleeping in a chair with a shotgun to drive off intruders intent on stripping the house. An agreement was made, whereby some land was sold for housing to provide income for the restoration, and the estate was given to the National Trust. Philip lived in a flat and often went out to chat to visitors until his death a few years later. Over the years the restoration has been gradual, even the garden being re-laid to the original plans.

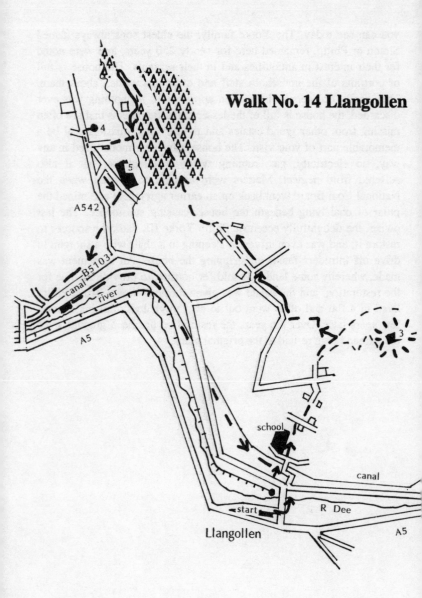

Walk No. 14 Llangollen

Llangollen – past and present

OS Map No.:	117
Start:	G.R. 214419 – main car park in town centre.
Access:	Llangollen lies between the A5 and the A439. Buses include National Express 521 (London); 94 Wrexham; 96 Oswestry.
Facilities:	Toilets in car park; full range of cafés etc. in town; information office.

Amount of climbing: 130m/430ft.

Llangollen is a small town with a lot to offer the visitor – music and dance (1); Dr Who and model trains; canal and railway rides; outstanding scenery and historical sites. This walk takes you to some of these through lovely countryside.

Walk Directions: (-) denotes Point of Interest

Turn right from the car park entrance, left at the main street, down it and over the River Dee by an old bridge (2). Cross the A539 and turn left. Within a few m/yards, turn right before the filling station at a brown signpost indicating a pedestrian route to the canal boats. Go right at the fork and up some steep steps. Cross the canal and go up the little steps directly opposite onto a tarmac path, signposted Castell Dinas Brân.

Your path is now uphill and is signposted, taking you through a kissing gate and over a lane; through another kissing gate onto a stony lane and over another crossing. At the third gate, do not follow the route signposted to the right to the castle, but continue straight ahead on a green path with the fence and trees on your left. Follow the path as it turns to the right, away from the fence, and shortly take a left fork and then another, and begin to go downhill. Above you now are the ruins of the castle (3) and in front the white limestone cliffs of

Creigiau Eglwyseg. The path drops, and when it meets the fence again turn, left. Cross a stile and turn right, following the fence and hedge on your right around the edge of the field to a stile and a lane. Turn right and follow the lane for about 440m/¼ mile, when it curves right at a junction and is signposted World's End, Minera.

In 90m/100 yards turn left up a drive signposted Tan y Fron. The path goes round the back of a house and over a signposted stile onto a green pathway, with superb views all round. A very gradual descent brings you to a junction with another path by a wire fence. Turn left so that you now walk in the opposite direction with the fence on your right. Cross a stile signposted on the right and just before some cottages, cross a stile on the left and follow a fence and hedge around the right side of the field. Go over an iron stile on the right signposted Velvet Hill, follow the path down, and cross the footbridge. Keep to the left of the field, cross a stile, and go up a track by a cottage, Pandy, to the road. You can see the Pillar of Eliseg (4) in a field to the right about 90m/100 yards away.

After visiting it, return, and turn left to the Abbey (5) passing the campsite shop. The Abbey entrance is on the left, and just past it a kissing gate on the right leads to a path going diagonally left to the road. Cross and turn left on the footpath for a short distance until you see a signpost on the right. A stile leads to a steep path which joins another. Turn left and you will find a signpost at the corner of a wood. Keep going, with the wood and fence on your left, climbing a little more at first before descending through bracken. Cross a stile into a wood and shortly you come out at a road.

Cross and go down the road opposite, signposted to Corwen. A short way down on the right there are toilets at the far end of a picnic area. Where the road bends right, there is a stone wall at the start of which a flight of stone steps leads down to an iron bridge over the canal. Turn right if you wish to see the Horseshoe Falls and the end of the canal, but turn left to continue the walk, passing the Chainbridge Hotel between the canal and the river. The towpath will bring you back to Llangollen.

Points of Interest:

(1) The International Music Eisteddfod has been held in the second week of July every year since its modest beginnings after WW II. For one week more than 12,000 participants and 150,000 spectators inundate the town which has population of only 3,000. Evening concerts feature stars such as Kennedy and Pavarotti who returned in 1995 to celebrate the 40th anniversary of his appearance in a male voice choir, but amateurs from all over the world dominate the week, and the massive organisation is still astonishingly run by a series of volunteer committees.

(2) The bridge over the River Dee is one of the Seven Wonders of Wales. Originally a packhorse bridge from the 14th century, it has been altered without losing its attractiveness. Its parapet is a wonderful viewpoint especially so in the autumn when canoe championships are held on the river.

(3) Castell Dinas Brân, not visited on this walk, stands 245m/800' above the town, and was recorded as lying in ruins in 1540. It was built in the early 13th century by Prince Madog ap Gruffydd Maelor on the site of an Iron Age fort. When Edward I attacked in his first campaign of 1277, the Welsh defenders retreated and destroyed the castle which was never re-built.

(4) The Pillar of Eliseg is what remains of a 9th century cross which gave its name to the area – Valle Crucis, the valley of the cross. It stands on a mound which contained a burial of the 6th or 7th century, but it is thought that the mound itself is prehistoric. The pillar is about 2.5m/8' high, but was originally about 6.25m/20'. It was pulled down and broken in the Civil War when the antiquary Edward Llwyd (see walk no. 6) was able to note its Latin inscription, now completely illegible. Its 31 lines of carving recorded the history of the royal house of Powys, the most detailed such record of its period. It was raised by Cyngen, the last king of Powys, who died in 854, and was in honour of his great-grandfather, Eliseg who 'united the inheritance of Powys out of the hand of the English with fire and sword'.

(5) Valley Crucis Abbey, founded in 1201, has a riverside setting

typical of those chosen by Cistercian, or 'white' monks from their clothing of undyed wool. Among the last to be built by the order, it was the first in the Gothic style. Remote locations were chosen by the Order so that the monks could more easily follow their austere way of life. Nevertheless, the monks here gained a reputation for good living, but managed to stay until the Dissolution in 1535, by which time the Commissioners reported that the abbey was 'in great decay'.

A few years later, part of the abbey became a private house, and in the 18th century most of the buildings were converted into a farm which it remained until restoration in the late 19th century. The west front is the part that you will see first. It has a carved doorway and a rose window with the inscription, 'Abbot Adam carried out this work; may he rest in peace. Amen.' The east end is equally striking, even today. Outside it is the monks' fishpond and six graves, among them, reputedly, that of Iolo Goch, the bard of Owain Glyndwr.

Pontcysyllte – ships in the sky

OS Map No.:	117
Start:	G.R. 282415 Ty Mawr Country Park
Access:	Ty Mawr is off the B5605, and is signposted from the A539, Ruabon to Llangollen road, Buses as for Llangollen.
Facilities:	Toilets, shop and refreshments in the country park and near the aqueduct.

Amount of climbing: 30m/100ft.

Ty Mawr is a country park oriented towards children and in itself worth a visit. The walk begins with 20 minutes on a B road made necessary by a lack of bridges in the right places for walkers! This is followed by a quiet stroll on the canal towpath and the highlight of the walk, the crossing of the Pontcysyllte aqueduct (1). The final leg is along the banks of the River Dee.

Walk Directions: (-) denotes Point of Interest

Go back to the road, turn right and pass under the railway arch. Cross the B5606 and go up Chapel Street opposite. Keep straight ahead and descend to the B road again. Cross and turn left using the footpath for 400m/¼ mile until you see the sign Pentre ¼. Cross again going past the war memorial. The road curves right by a letter box and passes the village school, before coming back again to the B road. Cross, turn left, and in a few m/yards turn right at a footpath sign onto the canal towpath. After a mile you reach a lift bridge. Here you can cross and turn left for the Aqueduct Inn on the A5, but our route stays on the towpath until you have crossed the Pontcysyllte Aqueduct, when you double back at the Offa's Dyke signpost onto a path which drops down to the arches of the aqueduct. (There are toilets on the right a little beyond the signpost, and refreshments just across the canal bridge.)

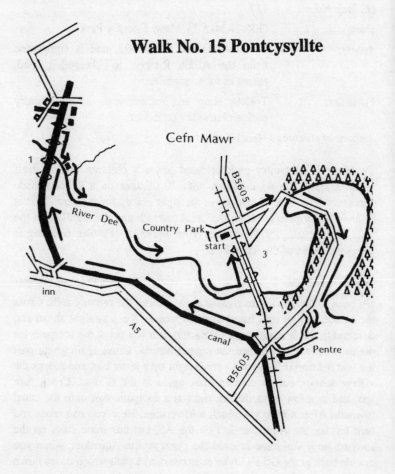

Walk No. 15 Pontcysyllte

Cefn Mawr

River Dee

Country Park
start

inn

canal

A5

B5605

B5605

Pentre

1

3

From here go down a long series of steps until you reach a well-constructed footpath by the river. Turn left and when you have crossed a bridge over a stream, follow the gravelled path on the right around the edge of a meadow.

A set of steps leads up into the country park and a junction with another path. Turn right to follow the path around the perimeter of the park, passing a picnic area by the river bank with a view of the viaduct (3). As you make your way back to the car park, do pause to look at the dovecote recently erected in memory of L/Cpl Edwards of the Royal Welch Fusiliers, who was killed while on peacekeeping duties with the UN in Bosnia in 1993.

Points of Interest:

(1) The aqueduct, designed by Thomas Telford (2) to carry the canal over the River Dee, opened almost 200 years ago. At 40m/130' above the river, and with a length of over 300/1000', it is a most impressive structure. It has 19 cast-iron arches, supported on hollow stone piers, the towpath on which you walk being cantilevered. If you lean over, you can see how the sections are fitted together like sections of a jigsaw puzzle.

It is recorded how in November 1805 a flotilla of boats crossed at the opening ceremony, one carrying the band of the Shropshire Volunteers to entertain the huge crowd, which had gathered to see these 'ships in the sky'.

(2) Thomas Telford's greatest influence on North Wales, though, is certainly his construction of the turnpike from London to Holyhead, now the A5, and still a major through route. The old stagecoach route had proved unsatisfactory, since the Act of Union with Ireland meant that MPs had regularly to travel between Dublin and London. Telford's route by-passed Llangollen, thus saving the old centre from development, and it went straight on through Snowdonia in a dramatic manner, passing the Nant-Ffrancon pass at Ogwen, and with a gradient that was never more than 1:20. The really breathtaking construction, though, must be the Menai suspension bridge linking Anglesey to the mainland, 30m/100' high and 180m/580' long.

Telford was a Scot apprenticed to a London stonemason who, having taught himself civil engineering, was appointed to the Ellesmere Canal Company, which was formed to join the rivers Mersey, Severn and Dee with a canal. It was his imaginative design for the Pontcysyllte aqueduct that earned him his reputation, and he went on to build not only the London-Holyhead turnpike, but other major engineering works such as St Katherine's Docks in London and the Caledonian Canal.

(3) The Cefn Viaduct was the work of Henry Robertson. Built in 1848 to carry the Chester-Shrewsbury railway, it has 19 arches, each with a span of 18m/60' and a height of 45m/147'.

Walks with History

If you want to experience the very best of Wales, then these are the books for you. The walks are graded and there is something for everybody – short walks for families and more demanding routes to satisfy even the most experienced hillwalker.

Whether you choose to walk the high grounds, explore the beautiful valleys, study the varied wildlife or visit the remains of ancient castles and forts, the points of interest will explain what makes each area unique and help you choose the right walk for you.

Walks on the Llŷn Peninsula
PART 1 - SOUTH & WEST – N. Burras & J. Stiff.
ISBN 0-86381-343-7; **£4.50**
This series combines walks with history, stories and legends. Pastoral walks as well as coastal & mountain panoramas.

Walks on the Llŷn Peninsula
PART 2 - NORTH & EAST – N. Burras & J. Stiff.
ISBN 0-86381-365-8; **£4.50**

Walks in the Snowdonia Mountains
– Don Hinson. 45 walks, mostly circular, 96 pages, inc. accurate maps and drawings. 96pp ISBN 0-86381-385-2; New Edition: **£3.75**

Walks in North Snowdonia
– Don Hinson. 100km of paths to help those wishing to explore the area further.
96pp ISBN 0-86381-386-0; New Edition; **£3.75**

New Walks in Snowdonia
– Don Hinson. 43 circular walks together with many variations. This book introduces you to lesser known paths and places which guide book writers seem to have neglected. Maps with every walk. Pen & ink drawings.
96pp ISBN 0-86381-390-9; New Edition; **£3.75**

Circular Walks in North Pembrokeshire
– Paul Williams, 14 walks, 112 pages. ISBN 0-86381-420-4; **£4.50**

Circular Walks in South Pembrokeshire
– Paul Williams, 14 walks, 120 pages. ISBN 0-86381-421-2; **£4.50**

From Mountain Tops to Valley Floors
Salter & Worral. ISBN 0-86381-430-1; **£4.50**
Detailed information for casual/family walks and for the more adventurous walker.